MW00651559

Screening Applicants for Effectiveness

SAFE

Guidelines to Prevent Child Molestation in Mentoring and Youth-Serving Organizations

Elsy Arévalo, B.A.
Daniel Chavira, M.D.
Becky Cooper, M.A., B.A.
Michelle Smith, M.P.A., B.A.

Friends for Youth, Inc.

Share. Enrich. Transform.

SAFE (Screening Applicants for Effectiveness): Guidelines to Prevent Child Molestation in Mentoring and Youth-Serving Organizations was developed and published by Friends for Youth, Inc., an organization dedicated to creating quality mentoring relationships for youth who need them most.

Published by:
Friends for Youth, Inc.

Written by:
Elsy Arévalo, B.A.
Daniel Chavira, M.D.
Becky Cooper, M.A., B.A.
Michelle Smith, M.P.A., B.A.

First Edition, Second Printing Edited by:
Becky Cooper, M.A., B.A.

First Edition, First Printing Edited by:
Michelle Smith, M.P.A., B.A.

Designed by:
Morris Jackson

Additional Image Design Elements by:
Yoshie Matsumoto, Melissa Tioleco-Cheng, and Robert J. Williams

Distributed by:
Friends for Youth, Inc., Redwood City, CA

First Edition, Second Printing Copyright © 2014 by Friends for Youth, Inc.
First Edition, First Printing Copyright © 2006 by Friends for Youth, Inc.

ISBN 978-0-692-36436-9

All rights reserved. No part of this book may be reproduced in any form or by any means without written permission from Friends for Youth, Inc.

Printed in the United States of America

SAFE is one of the most comprehensive and scholarly publications that addresses the need to ensure maximum protection for individuals involved in mentoring programs. The document will serve well to guide professionals in the field of mentoring.

Dr. Susan G. Weinberger
President, Mentor Consulting Group

Table of Contents

This volume should not be viewed as the rendering of legal advice, and programs are strongly encouraged to consult their legal counsel prior to implementing the recommendations found in this manual.

Foreword

What an honor it has been for me to have been part of an incredible mentoring community – a true community of caring for children and youth. My mentoring journey began in 1979 when I was hired as the first Program Coordinator for an emerging program in the San Francisco Bay Area. The seemingly simple concept of providing a caring adult friend to a youth-in-need struck a chord with me, but I immediately learned that it was not as simple as it appeared.

I was tasked with matching vulnerable youth one-on-one with adult volunteers who would serve as mentors and build relationships with them. As I first endeavored to interview and vet potential mentors, however, I was occasionally struck with an uneasiness or discomfort with an individual that I could not attribute to any specific event or knowledge that I had. I just knew that, given the choice, I was not comfortable matching them with our children. Then, every once in awhile, I would see a small article in the back pages of a newspaper stating that someone had been charged with molesting a child in a youth-service setting.

Thus began my extensive search to find out how I could identify these potential predators who were looking to meet youth through our organization. The subject of child predators is an uncomfortable topic, and there was a pervasive lack of knowledge on the subject. Although it may be difficult, *it is a necessary conversation*. Building on the work of Dr. A. Nicolas Groth, expertise provided by Sergeant Ted Marfia of the San Jose Police Department's Child Exploitation Unit, and countless reviews of profiles of volunteers who were rejected by mentoring agencies, the need to compile and share this crucial information became apparent to me. As such, *SAFE* was launched.

There is greater awareness of this issue today. The Jerry Sandusky case at Penn State in 2011 brought the subject of child predators squarely in the public consciousness, and the demand for information soared. This is our second printing of *SAFE*, and Friends for Youth has trained thousands of youth-serving professionals on this topic.

It has indeed been a privilege for me to have helped create impactful, life-long relationships that have touched the lives of both the mentees and their mentors. It is my most fervent hope that the information provided by *SAFE* will continue to help youth-serving agencies, along with parents and community members, become knowledgeable and proficient about keeping our children and youth safe.

Becky Cooper

Executive Director
Friends for Youth, Inc.

About Friends for Youth

Friends for Youth's mentoring services expertly facilitates and supports deep and trusting, long term, one-to-one friendships between youth-in-need and adult mentors that positively impact both parties and the entire community. Friends for Youth's decades of service, expertise and leadership in its field enables its Mentoring Institute to help millions of at-risk youth around the world through education and recommended best practices.

Friends for Youth was established in 1979 by local community leaders, including the Director of Juvenile Probation, who recognized that many at-risk children did not fit the focus of other available services. Since its inception, Friends for Youth has worked to support children who would otherwise go unserved, with an emphasis on positive youth development, academic achievement, health and wellness, prevention services, and critical skills for future self-sufficiency.

Friends for Youth has matched 2,000 youth with caring mentors, providing ongoing follow-up support, life skills education, and community activities and opportunities. Friends for Youth has achieved a 90% average success rate of creating long-term, community-based, one-to-one friendships, a percentage significantly higher than the 33-67% rate cited in Marc Freedman's *The Kindness of Strangers* for similar programs nationwide.[1] Youth are low-income, diverse, and are referred to Friends for Youth for being at risk of or involved with abuse and violence, academic failure, or substance abuse. Friends for Youth has been called the "gold standard" in the mentoring field by leading researcher Dr. Jean Rhodes.

---

[1] Freedman, Marc. (1993). The Kindness of Strangers. San Francisco, CA: Jossey-Bass Publishers. Pp. 77-80.

Friends for Youth's Mentoring Institute began in 1998 with seed money from the David and Lucile Packard Foundation, as a response to the growing number of programs beginning across the nation and the need for standardized recommended best practices in mentoring our youth. Friends for Youth shares its expertise in the mentoring field based on decades of successful programming.

Acknowledgements

The issue of child molestation seems so dark and can make us feel so helpless that it is difficult to imagine goodness associated with it. In writing this manual, however, we uncovered significant hope as we engaged in research and discussions with individuals and organizations dedicated to keeping children safe. This manual was greatly enriched by their contributions: their insights are sprinkled throughout this manual and add depth to the topics of child molestation, mentoring, and volunteer management. We would like to acknowledge and thank them for their contributions to this manual and, more importantly, for their dedication to enriching the lives of youth throughout our communities:

Dave Allburn, former Director, Safe Harbor Resources, Glouster, OH

Veronica Blaustein, former Access Programs Associate, 1000 Degrees, San Rafael, CA

Rebecca Duran, Mentoring Services Director, Friends for Youth, Inc., Redwood City, CA

Kathryn M. Eustis, Director, Youth Development and Prevention Programs, Calaveras Youth Mentoring Program, Angels Camp, CA

Whitney Gabriel, National Director, Child Safety, Abel Screening, Inc., Alameda, CA

Marie Gelineau, Executive Director, Three River Valley Business and Education Partnership, Springfield, VT

Lorey Keele, Community Programs Director, Redwood Community Action Agency, Eureka, CA

Sarah Kremer, former Mentoring Institute Director, Friends for Youth, Inc., Redwood City, CA

Heather Laird, former Mentoring Institute Consultant, Friends for Youth, Inc., Redwood City, CA

Steven McEwan, Sergeant, San Jose Police Department, San Jose, CA

John Patterson, Senior Program Director, Nonprofit Risk Management Center, Washington, DC

Dr. Perry Sirota, Director, Sirota Psychological Services, Calgary, Alberta, Canada

Andrew Vachss, Attorney, Consultant, and Founder of Protect, New York, NY

Lynne West, Chief Executive Officer, Big Brothers Big Sisters of Ventura County, Ventura, CA

Karen Wilmer, Associate Director, Friends for Youth, Inc., Redwood City, CA

Introduction

"The only responsibility that a man cannot evade in this life is the one he probably thinks of least – his personal influence. ... Every moment of life he is changing, to a degree, the life of the whole world."[2]

The primary duty of youth service providers is to care for the well-being, healthy development, and growth of children. The field of mentoring seeks to fulfill this duty by connecting children with adults to help them see that their life matters, to provide them with a model for a healthy relationship, to show them that they have valuable gifts to share with others, and to illustrate through action that someone cares deeply about their well-being. Mentoring seeks to connect youth with caring individuals who will be present on a consistent basis and will help open up their minds and hearts to the opportunities available in the world.[3] At the core of the mentoring movement is the fundamental belief that human relationships have the power to change, heal, and nurture. Research into the effects of mentoring has confirmed this intuitive truth: human beings thrive under supportive relationships.

Unfortunately, the corollary is also true: human relationships have the power to impede growth and even to damage. Specifically, research has shown that mentoring practices which lead to disappointing relationships can have adverse effects on youth, eroding their self-esteem and trust in adults.[4] One type of relationship which has been shown to have powerfully negative effects on the growth and development of children is that of

[2] Jordan, William George. (1980). *The Majesty of Calmness.* Center City, MN: Hazelden Publishing and Educational Services.
[3] Governor's Mentoring Partnership. (2002, September). Recommended Best Practices for Mentor Programs. Retrieved November 25, 2005, from http://www.mentoring.ca.gov/best_practices.shtm.
[4] Rhodes, Jean E. (2002). *Stand by Me: The Risks and Rewards of Mentoring Today's Youth.* Cambridge, MA: Harvard University Press.

sexual abuse. Our goal in writing this manual is to provide youth service providers with the knowledge necessary to prevent this form of abuse within their organizations. It is important to understand the issue of child sexual abuse because mentoring programs are inherently vulnerable to this threat. Mentoring brings adult volunteers into contact with vulnerable children. In one-to-one mentoring, classroom guidance, or even in online communication, the creation of a relationship between a child and an adult establishes a line of communication which can be used to harm children. The very nature of our business demands that we match volunteers with children and encourage them to establish trust, break down natural barriers of "stranger" caution, and create an opportunity for abuse. It is in this type of relationship that child sexual abuse thrives.

The practice of mentoring is filled with challenges which can make us inclined to take what we can get, do what we can, and hope for the best. While doing what we can, however, we must remember that the old saying "doing something is better than doing nothing at all" is untrue when it comes to mentoring youth. Our first principle must be "do no harm." It is vital that we are informed and educated on the inherent risks in the relationships we create.

Project Relevance

Each year, nearly 35 million adults come in contact with more than 80 million young people through activities provided by organizations serving children and youth. Many, if not most, of the adults involved in mentoring programs are given the mandate to build close and positive mentoring relationships with youth.[5] The vast majority of volunteers become involved because they want to do just that. However, within any pool of potential volunteers, there exists a portion of individuals who specifically target youth-serving organizations with the hope and goal to sexually abuse children. As you will learn in this manual, there are organizations which actively support sexual relationships between children and adults. Some of their websites go so far as to list organizations which can connect molesters with young targets. Included on these lists are mentoring agencies, schools, and other youth-serving organizations.

However shocking or repulsive, this form of organized and unorganized predatory behavior exists, and youth service providers must be aware of these risks if they are to

---

[5] Office of Juvenile Justice and Delinquency Prevention. (1998, April). Guidelines for the Screening of Persons Working with Children, the Elderly, and Individuals with Disabilities in Need of Support. Retrieved November 25, 2005, from http://ojjdp.ncjrs.org/pubs/guidelines/contents.html.

safeguard children. Research supports the necessity of thoroughly and carefully screening and monitoring all volunteers.

It is generally accepted that over 90% of all child molesters are known to their victims.[6] The old belief that we need only to worry about protecting children from the "dirty old man lurking nearby" is both outdated and horribly misleading. Those who pose the greatest danger are typically individuals whom children know and associate with on a regular basis. They include family members, teachers, coaches, neighbors, volunteers, other authority figures, and even other youth. These individuals seek to have as many opportunities as possible to gain access to children. And many of these perpetrators have molested hundreds of victims by the time they are caught.[7]

The number of victimized children is not small or insignificant. Research conducted by the Centers for Disease Control estimates that approximately 1 in 6 boys and 1 in 4 girls are sexually abused before the age of 18.[8] This abuse is associated with a multitude of negative consequences ranging from depression and suicidal ideology to post-traumatic stress disorders and arrested development.[9] [10] [11] The role of mentoring organizations is therefore critical in protecting children from the shame, guilt, and multitude of problems associated with child sexual abuse. This manual was written to provide information and tools needed to prevent child molestation by effectively screening and monitoring volunteers.

---

[6] de Becker, Gavin. (1997). *The Gift of Fear*. New York, NY: Dell Publishing. P.15.
[7] Abel, G., Becker, J., Mittleman, M., Rouleau, J., and Murphy, W. (1987). Self-reported sex crimes of nonincarcerated paraphiliacs. *Journal of Interpersonal Violence*, 2(1), March. Pp. 3-25.
[8] "Child Sexual Abuse: What Parents Should Know." American Psychological Association. http://apa.org/pi/families/resources/child-sexual-abuse.aspx. February 19, 2014
[9] van Dam, Carla. (2001). *Identifying Child Molesters: Preventing Child Sexual Abuse*. New York, NY: Haworth Maltreatment and Trauma Press. p. 60.
[10] Abel, Gene G. and Harlow, Nora. (2001). *The Stop Child Molestation Book: What Ordinary People Can Do In Their Everyday Lives to Save Three Million Children*. Philadelphia, PA: Xlibris. P. 29.
[11] Putnam, Frank. (1998). *Why is it so Difficult for the Epidemic of Child Abuse to be Taken Seriously?* [Transcript] David L. Chadwick Endowed Lecture, San Diego Conference on Responding to the Maltreatment of Children, January 30, 1998.

Letter from a Mentoring Program

I would like to take this opportunity to talk about mentor/mentee matches. Our mentoring program has endeavored for the past three years to match at-risk youth with adult mentors. We matched our city official with a highly at-risk youth. The match initially showed signs of being a good one. The youth's overall behavior changed for the better. He started focusing on how he might be able to contribute to society. He got involved in youth projects. He was instrumental in the new Skateboard Park Project. He was the spokesperson at numerous meetings. The City Council approved the project. I remember an old saying, "All that glitters is not gold." This young man's behavior began to change. Due to confidentiality, I cannot reveal all the things that happened. The behavior of the mentor apparently changed as well. The end result was an allegation of child molestation. The mentor was convicted and sent to jail. We lost a number of mentors. They were reluctant to continue mentoring because of all the negative publicity. Our program learned a lot from this situation. Even though there may be lingering effects, we have bounced back. So, my question to all programs would be, "What's considered a good match - do you know all there is to know about your mentors?"

SAFE was created on the premise that action without knowledge can be dangerous, even with the best intentions. This manual attempts to provide youth service providers and, more specifically, mentoring staff with the knowledge necessary to help inform their judgment as they screen and monitor their volunteers. Although there have been significant advances in the research of child sexual abuse, little of this information specifically addresses the needs of mentoring organizations. This is the first publication of accepted, clear, and consistent guidelines for mentoring agencies to utilize in identifying potential child predators within their programs. This book seeks to combine the latest research on child sexual abuse with the experience and knowledge of Friends for Youth, Inc.

This volume offers statistics on the prevalence of sexual abuse, characteristics of child molesters, their grooming tactics, and information on victims, as well as guidelines which can help protect youth in mentoring organizations. This publication is not intended to be an all-encompassing or groundbreaking study of pedophilia, its etiology, typology, or treatment options. It has been written to provide both a literature review of background information and practical advice on screening and monitoring volunteers to prevent abuse. While this material may apply to any youth-serving organization, it is specifically designed to respond to the needs of mentoring programs.

This *SAFE* manual has been divided into three main sections. Part I is a literature review of the latest child molestation research. This section details the prevalence and impact of child molestation, with profiles of victims and perpetrators and the dynamics of abuse. Part II highlights the integration of this information into each facet of a mentoring program, detailing mentor screening tools, the use of Informed Intuition, and child predator red flags. Finally, Part III offers tools and resources for the application of the guidelines presented in this manual. Throughout the manual, reflection questions, scenarios, and open-ended content are offered to help staff deepen their understanding of issues as they relate to each program's unique needs. *SAFE* **should not be viewed as the rendering of legal advice, and programs are strongly encouraged to consult their legal counsel prior to implementing the recommendations found in this manual.** It is our hope that the information provided will assist programs in managing the risk inherent in their services, supporting their ability to fulfill their mission for years to come. Most importantly, we hope this manual helps to create caring, trusting, and safe relationships for youth who need them most.

Research into the effectiveness of educating children or parents on child molestation prevention has provided varying and sometimes conflicting results.[12][13] Perhaps our best educational tool in the prevention of child sexual abuse, therefore, is training all staff members on the dynamics of abuse and indicators which may be observed when screening and monitoring volunteers. Without this education, staff members may lack the knowledge necessary to recognize warning signs or validate their intuitive feelings about a particular volunteer. All staff working to connect children with mentors should be trained in the definitions of child sexual abuse, the prevalence and effects of abuse, information about victims and perpetrators, the dynamics of abuse, sample case studies, red flags and warning signs, and screening and monitoring steps which prevent abuse. The issue of educating staff is critical, particularly in considering the high turnover rates within the mentoring industry. Staff education can balance the pressure of making matches quickly with the importance of quality matches. Additionally, reviewing

---

[12] Repucci, N.D., Land, D., and Haugaard, J. (1998). Child Sexual Abuse Prevention Programs that Target Young Children. In *Violence against Children in the Family and Community*. Trickett, P.K. and Schellenbach, C.J. (Eds.), Washington, DC: American Psychological Association.
[13] Kolko, D. J. (1988). Educational programs to promote awareness and prevention of child sexual victimization: A review and methodological critique. *Clinical Psychology Review*, 8, 195-209.

information on child abuse prevention will emphasize that the healthy and safe development of children is an organization's number one priority.

It is important to note that we realize this is an extremely uncomfortable topic. In our experience as training and consultation providers, we have learned that child sexual abuse is an issue that most individuals prefer not to consider, much less study. It often generates anxiety and fear about the potential danger for youth and the liabilities for an organization. Some individuals do not like "dwelling" on the topic, perhaps because they do not believe it is a problem or because they cannot believe that anyone would want to sexually molest a child. Tragically, denial is a "save-now-pay-later scheme."[14] We hope that, at the very least, readers will entertain the notion that it is possible for a child molester to apply to and infiltrate your program. Denial will blind you. Information will alert you to potential danger.

"In the United States, society's historical attitude
about sexual victimization of children
*can generally be summed up in one word: **denial**."*[15]

"As long as we have a nationwide failure to know
the most basic facts about our molested children and their molesters,
every child is at risk."[16]

[14] de Becker, Gavin. (1997). *The Gift of Fear*. New York, NY: Dell Publishing. P. 10.
[15] Lanning, Kenneth V. (2010) *Child Molesters: A Behavioral Analysis*. U.S. Department of Justice.
[16] Abel, Gene G. and Harlow, Nora. (2001). *The Stop Child Molestation Book: What Ordinary People Can Do In Their Everyday Lives to Save Three Million Children*. Philadelphia, PA: Xlibris.

Glossary of Terms

*"What people think sexual abuse is
and how seriously they take it
affects how they behave."*[17]

O ne of the first hurdles found in the research and in any discussion about child molestation is a lack of consistent definitions regarding what exactly constitutes child molestation and, most importantly, what constitutes a child. The term "child molestation" leads to the exploration of related terms. The variety and use of these terms are related to the myriad of disciplines attempting to understand, study, predict, prevent, and sometimes even advocate for child molestation. Some definitions have to do with the law; these are based on criminal behavior and on what is considered legal or illegal. Other definitions are psychiatric in nature and are geared toward classification for treatment purposes.

In approaching this topic, we must contend with the inherent deficiencies and confusion created by the use of different terms, as well as the myriad of images, ideas, emotions, and perceptions we each bring to the conversation. Misconceptions or stereotypes of child molesters may prevent us from seeing the young college student, the president of a company, or the upstanding community member as possible perpetrators. Clearly, before we begin a discussion on child molestation, it is important that we speak the same language. What follows is a list of the most relevant terms and definitions used in this study of child molestation.

---

[17] Finkelhor, David. (1984). *Child Sexual Abuse: New Theory and Research.* New York, NY: Free Press. P. 107.

- **Boylover/Girllover:** Terms used by pedophiles to describe their gender preference for either boys or girls. It is important, however, to note that pedophiles are often sexually attracted to, and can act upon their sexual urges for, both boys and girls.

- **Child:** To define a child we will borrow the legal definition. A child is an individual who has not yet reached his or her 18th birthday.

- **Child Abuse:** Any act (or failure to act) which results in death, serious physical or emotional harm, sexual abuse, or exploitation.[18]

- **Child Sexual Abuse:** Sexual activities involving a child intended for sexual stimulation. These activities cover the spectrum from exhibitionism and voyeurism to fondling or penetration. This abuse includes violation of a trusting relationship with unequal power and/or advanced knowledge. Abusive activities are carried out using secrecy, force, or trickery.[19][20]

- **Child Molester:** Any adult or child, male or female, known or unknown, who is at least 5 years older than the child he or she has sexually abused.[21]

- **Child Predator:** An adult whose primary sexual interests lie with children (persons under 18 years of age).[22]

- **Ephebophile/Ephebophilia:** An ephebophile is an individual who is affected with ephebophilia, a sexual attraction to young people about the age of puberty (post-pubertal adolescents [ages 14-17]).[23] Within this manual, child predators will include those affected with either pedophilia or ephebophilia.

---

[18] National Clearinghouse on Child Abuse and Neglect Information. (2005). *Definitions of Child Abuse and Neglect: Summary of State Laws.* Washington, DC: National Clearinghouse on Child Abuse and Neglect Information. Retrieved December 5, 2005, from http://nccanch.acf.hhs.gov/general/legal/statutes/defineall.pdf.

[19] van Dam, Carla. (2001). *Identifying Child Molesters: Preventing Child Sexual Abuse.* New York, NY: Haworth Maltreatment and Trauma Press. P. 50.

[20] Finkelhor, David. (1994). Current Information on the Scope and Nature of Child Sexual Abuse. From *The Future of Children* (4)2, a publication of the David and Lucile Packard Foundation. P. 33. Retrieved on November 25, 2005, from http://www.futureofchildren.org/usr_doc/vol4no2ART2.pdf.

[21] Lanning, Charles. (2001). *Child Molesters: A Behavioral Analysis.* Washington, DC: United States Department of Justice. P. 15.

[22] McEwan, Steven. Child Sexual Exploitation. (2002). California's San Jose Police Department, Child Exploitation Detail (unpublished manuscript). P. 4.

[23] American Psychiatric Association. (2000) *Diagnostic and Statistical Manual of Mental Disorders (4th ed./text revision).* Washington, DC: American Psychiatric Association.

- **Incest:** When a child is molested by a family member (e.g., brother, father, or aunt).

- **Paraphilia:** A psychosexual disorder or sexual deviation characterized by fantasies, behaviors, or sexual urges focusing on unusual objects, activities, or situations. Some common paraphilias include exhibitionism, voyeurism, masochism, and pedophilia.[24]

- **Pedophile/Pedophilia:** A pedophile is an individual who is affected with pedophilia, a condition met by the following criteria:[25]
  Criterion A: Over a period of at least 6 months, [this person has] recurrent, intense sexually arousing fantasies, sexual urges, or behaviors involving sexual activity with a prepubescent child or children (generally age 13 years or younger).
  Criterion B: The fantasies, sexual urges, or behaviors cause clinically significant distress or impairment in social, occupational, or other important areas of functioning.
  Criterion C: The person is at least age 16 years of age and at least 5 years older than the child or children in Criterion A.

While the media and many lay people use the term "pedophilia" interchangeably with "child molestation," there are important distinctions. Within the American Psychiatric Association's *Diagnostic and Statistical Manual of Mental Disorders (DSM-IV-TR)*, the definition of "pedophilia" is intended to be used by psychologists for classification of treatment purposes, and the absence of any of the key criteria could technically eliminate the diagnosis. For instance, a person can be a pedophile without ever having molested a child (i.e., if they just have urges or fantasies to molest but have never acted on those urges). Or, more interestingly, an individual can molest a child without being a pedophile (i.e., in the case of someone who molests a child without having recurrent, intense sexual fantasies involving children). There is also significant discussion regarding the criteria that an individual must be at least 16 years of age to be considered a pedophile. Research has shown that many child molesters begin fantasizing about sexual relations with younger children and act upon those urges at an early age. As one

---

[24] American Psychiatric Association. (2000) *Diagnostic and Statistical Manual of Mental Disorders (4th ed./text revision)*. Washington, DC: American Psychiatric Association.
[25] American Psychiatric Association. (2000) *Diagnostic and Statistical Manual of Mental Disorders (4th ed./text revision)*. Washington, DC: American Psychiatric Association.

self-labeled pedophile explains, "... Why all the reluctance to assign pedophilia to younger people? Most of the research suggests that sexual preferences (including pedophilia) are set at a fairly young age. Certainly, in my own case, I know I was attracted to children basically since puberty."[26] Technically, an individual would also not be considered a pedophile if they have intense fantasies and urges involving children, but they are fantasies of post-pubertal children. Thus the need for the term "ephebophilia" (above).

- Sex Offender: Typically used within a legal context, this is a broadly-used term which refers to those who offend against adult victims, child victims, or both.[27]

---

[26] Retrieved November 25, 2005, from http://www.paedosexualitaet.de/lib/DSM-IV1994.html.

[27] Becker, J. and Skinner, L. (1994). Behavioral treatment of sexual dysfunctions in sexual assault survivors. In I.R. Stuart and J.G. Greer (Eds.), *Victims of sexual aggression: Treatment of children, women and men* (pp. 211-233). New York, NY: Van Nostrand Reinhold Company.

PART I
Child Molestation: A Literature Review

There is a significant and growing amount of research, articles, and initiatives on the topic of child molestation. Because we realize that it is impossible to expect youth service providers to read all available information, we have attempted to include summaries of only the most relevant material. Our goal in developing this section was not to merely report information. Instead, we have attempted to analyze these details from the perspective of a youth-serving organization, highlighting those topics, ideas, and questions which would most benefit the mentoring and youth-serving community.

CHAPTER 1:
The Prevalence and Impact of Child Molestation

Sex crimes are unfortunately fairly common in the United States. Approximately 1 in 6 boys and 1 in 4 girls are sexually abused before the age of 18.[28]

There is a good deal of discussion and controversy over the prevalence of child molestation. Some individuals choose to ignore recent data, feeling it is simply another issue over-hyped by modern media. Others actively try to downplay its significance, concerned about the effects that defining the problem may have on their business, their organization, or their own actions. Still other well-meaning individuals choose to exaggerate the rates of abuse in an attempt to call people to action. Current research continues to explore the prevalence of child sexual abuse, offering insight into the nature and urgency of the issue.

For a number of reasons, it is difficult to ascertain the actual number of individuals who have been sexually abused. This difficulty comes principally from the reluctance of victims to share their abuse. Many victims, especially boys, do not disclose. Many victims choose never to tell anyone about their molestation due to the shame, guilt, and fear associated with being a victim of sexual abuse.

---

[28] "Child Sexual Abuse: What Parents Should Know." American Psychological Association. http://apa.org/pi/families/resources/child-sexual-abuse.aspx. February 19, 2014.

The organization STOP IT NOW! conducted a survey soliciting information from approximately one thousand survivors of child sexual abuse. They found that a staggering 91% of these survivors did not disclose the abuse when it was happening.[29] It is not difficult to understand why this is the case. Children often feel at fault for the molestation and can try to hide actions which they perceive as their wrongdoing. An interview with one survivor of child molestation reveals the mindset of many victims: "I just thought I was doing something bad. It was kind of like reading pornography or masturbating ... there's no way I would have told my parents or anyone else. Even now, it's difficult to admit that I learned to read porn from my molester. It seemed like my natural curiosity, my action. Of course, I was six years old, but I felt I was making the choice. When he began to touch me, it felt like he was just extending the education and I was choosing to go on with it."[30]

In addition to this lack of disclosure by victims, there are also many societal barriers to acknowledging abuse and the potential for abuse. In her book *Identifying Child Molesters*, Dr. Carla van Dam notes several instances in which communities or groups have gone to great lengths to avoid acknowledging molesters among them. Many parents, for example, can turn a blind eye to an adult spending undue time with their child because they are grateful for the help. Many child molesters begin their relationships with small acts of kindness which endear them to both parents and children. Their initial actions often build trust and break down walls of suspicion. It is hard to blame parents for allowing a neighbor, family member, or friend to pick up their children from school, spend time with them on weekends, or invite them along on social functions. While these may be natural aspects of societal living, it is by tapping into family needs that molesters are able to begin relationships with their victims. Once these relationships are established, it is often difficult for society to acknowledge that sexual abuse could be taking place. It is because of these circumstances and vulnerabilities that child molesters can continue to act. It is because of societal blindness that the actual prevalence of abuse is so hard to define.

Another confounding factor in the study of prevalence of childhood sexual abuse is the legal justice system. This system permits many perpetrators to go free so as not to punish one innocently-accused individual. Much of the available information

---

[29] Henry, Fran. The Impact of Sexual Abuse and its Implications for Our Work. STOP IT NOW! Opening Plenary Speech, U.S. Department of Justice Office of Justice Programs Second National Summit: Promoting Public Safety through Sexual Assault Prevention and Sex Offender Management. Washington, DC. December 17-19, 2000.

[30] Victim interview (personal correspondence, 2004).

Turning a Blind Eye

Perhaps one of the most notable instances of an organization turning a blind eye to abuse is demonstrated by the child molestation scandal within the Catholic Church of America. In this setting, church officials, parishioners, parents, and children managed to turn a blind eye to the actions of child molesters for years. Only once a brave few came out with the abuse did the extent of the problem become revealed. However, it is important to note that what initially may have appeared to be a sudden explosion and rise of child abuse cases within the church is more likely a result of years of concealment and a set of conditions which seem to be the ideal setting for abuse. The child molesters in this scenario were all offered blind, unquestioned, and complete access to children.

But religious organizations are not the only ones who should be concerned about this issue. The cycle of abuse can also remain hidden and can even be perpetuated by our very industry. It is not difficult to see why and how a child molester could infiltrate a youth service organization:

- Youth service organizations, by their very mission, target a molester's ideal victims: children.
- Organizations may inadvertently assist molesters by helping to gain the trust of parents and by serving to legitimize the relationship.
- Many programs do not have strong screening and monitoring processes in place. What time is there? Organizations need more volunteers, not less. Youth service providers, charged with making "matches" and placing volunteers to work with the youth, often feel pressured to reach quotas and serve a specific number of youth.
- Many youth service providers charged with managing volunteers receive very little training on child abuse prevention.
- The turnover rates in the mentoring industry are high, making it very difficult to provide ongoing, continuous supervision to volunteers.
- Finally, it is difficult to learn from other organizations that have experienced child abuse allegations as these organizations may choose to conceal the abuse for fear of potential liability and loss of credibility.

about the scope of this problem is gathered from the criminal justice system or Child Protective Services. These sources are inherently limited because they require that either a victim comes forward or a molester is caught in the act – both of which are rare events. The process also requires that formal charges are filed. Ultimately, the majority of victims never tell, so the majority of molesters are never caught. Detectives from the Child Exploitation Unit of California's San Jose Police Department have confirmed that by the time a child molester is caught, he or she has left behind a trail of victims.[31] Researcher Gene Abel reports that only "one in 150 deviant episodes actually leads to arrest," let alone conviction.[32] Furthermore, studies indicate that even when reports are made, the charges are often dropped, and even if a child molester is convicted, he will quickly be reintroduced to society due to lenient sentencing.[33] One study found that only 42% of sexual abuse allegations substantiated by child protection authorities were actually forwarded to prosecution. Even more disturbing is the fact that, even if they are tried and convicted, 32% to 46% of convicted abusers receive no jail time, and only 19% receive sentences longer than a year.[34] Such individuals are soon back in the community.

It is clear that many offenders go undetected and unreported,[35] making it difficult to discern the exact incidence of child sexual molestation. It has become increasingly clear, however, that the prevalence is startlingly high and the effects are devastatingly real. During this year alone, tens of thousands of boys and girls will be sexually abused. This information can be gathered through one of the most reliable sources of annual incidence of child sexual abuse, the National Incidence Study (NIS). The NIS is a congressionally mandated, federally funded report of child abuse and neglect. This periodic effort of the National Center on Child Abuse and Neglect (NCCAN) helps to define the extent and influence of child abuse. There have been 4 such studies conducted to date. The latest study, published in 2010, is the NIS-4. This was conducted in a nationally representative sample of 11,321 professionals in 1,094 agencies serving 122 counties. NIS figures are important because they include both children investigated by child protective service (CPS) agencies, as well as cases reported by psychologists,

[31] McEwan, Steven. San Jose Police Department, Child Exploitation Unit (personal correspondence 2004).
[32] Abel, G., Becker, J., Mittleman, M., Rouleau, J., and Murphy, W. (1987). Self-reported sex crimes of nonincarcerated paraphiliacs. *Journal of Interpersonal Violence*, 2(1), March. Pp. 3-25.
[33] Finkelhor, David. (1994). *Current Information on the Scope and Nature of Child Sexual Abuse*. From *The Future of Children (4)2*, a publication of the David and Lucile Packard Foundation. P. 45. Retrieved on November 25, 2005, from http://www.futureofchildren.org/usr_doc/vol4no2ART2.pdf.
[34] Finkelhor, David. (1994). Current Information on the Scope and Nature of Child Sexual Abuse. From *The Future of Children (4)2*, a publication of the David and Lucile Packard Foundation. P. 31-53. Retrieved on November 25, 2005, from http://www.futureofchildren.org/usr_doc/vol4no2ART2.pdf
[35] Abel, Gene G. and Harlow, Nora. (2001). *The Stop Child Molestation Book: What Ordinary People Can Do In Their Everyday Lives to Save Three Million Children*. Philadelphia, PA: Xlibris. P. 23.

psychiatrists, youth professionals, and other mandated reporters. Two sets of standards are applied in deriving estimates for the study: the Harm Standard and the Endangerment Standard.

The Harm Standard is more stringent: this requires that an act or omission resulted in demonstrable harm. Though highly objective, the Harm Standard has the primary disadvantage of providing a very conservative view of abuse and neglect. Nonetheless, under the Harm Standard, the estimated number of sexually abused children in the course of a year was 135,300, or 24% of the estimated 1.25 million children experiencing maltreatment during the study.

The second measure, the Endangerment Standard, allows children who were not yet harmed by maltreatment to be counted in the abused and neglected estimates. Under the Endangerment Standard, the estimated number of sexually abused children per year was 180,500, or 22% of the 3 million children who experienced maltreatment.[36] This means that this year alone, hundreds of thousands of children will be damaged physically, mentally, and emotionally. Although high, these numbers only tell us how many children were sexually victimized during the course of one year. They do not indicate the overall number of victims who were sexually abused as children.

Another way in which researchers have been able to come to understand the scope of the problem is to look at retrospective studies of adults. Researchers Peters, Wyatt, and Finkelhor gathered and compiled 19 such retrospective studies of adults completed in the United States and Canada since 1980.[37] They found considerable evidence to show that at least 20% of American women and 5% to 16% of American men experienced some form of sexual abuse as children. The authors note that it is generally believed that respondents are likely to under-report their abuse due to embarrassment or privacy concerns. Most reviewers, however, do conclude that at least 1 out of every 4 women and 1 out of every 6 men have been sexually abused as children.[38] [39]

---

[36] Sedlack, Andrea et. al. Fourth National Incidence Study of Child Abuse and Neglect (NIS-4) Report to Congress. January 2010. Retrieved on January 6, 2014 from www.acf.hhs.gov/sites/default/opre/nis4_report_congress_full
[37] Peters, S.D., Wyatt, G.E., and Finkelhor, D. (1986). Prevalence. In D. Finkelhor (Ed.), *Understanding and Managing Child Sexual Abuse* (pp. 15-59). Beverly Hills, CA: Sage.
[38] "Child Sexual Abuse: What Parents Should Know." American Psychological Association. http://apa.org/pi/families/resources/child-sexual-abuse.aspx. February 19, 2014
[39] Abel, Gene G. and Harlow, Nora. (2001). *The Stop Child Molestation Book: What Ordinary People Can Do In Their Everyday Lives to Save Three Million Children*. Philadelphia, PA: Xlibris. P. 20.

Impact of Childhood Sexual Abuse

"Failure to understand the impact of abuse on children
interferes with properly managing events preceding the molest."[40]

Like the prevalence of sexual abuse, the harm of child sexual abuse is difficult to measure. However, the preponderance of evidence links childhood sexual abuse to a variety of psychiatric, physical, and developmental issues including Post-Traumatic Stress Disorder, sexually transmitted diseases, teen pregnancy, increased drug and alcohol use, obsessive-compulsive disorder, depression, personality disorders, increased suicidality, increased prevalence of parenting difficulties, increased utilization of health and social services, high cost of lost work days, psychiatric issues, and interference with the normal development of adult sexual behavior.[41][42] The extent of the psychological, emotional, and physical effects depends on a number of variables, including the support systems available to the child prior, during, and after the abuse.[43] Other factors include the circumstances, severity, and frequency of the abuse.[44] While untangling the specific effects of abuse is more appropriate to dedicated psychological research, it is clear that child sexual abuse is an important, independent risk factor for psychological, physical, emotional, and interpersonal hardship.[45] This hardship presents a problem not only to the individual but also to the community which must deal with the loss of work hours, increased health costs, potential continuation of the cycle of abuse, and even increased institutional costs in hospitals, rehabilitation centers, or prisons. As explained by Charles Lanning, "Sadly, one of the main reasons why the criminal justice system and the public were forced to confront the problem of molestation was the preponderance of lawsuits arising from the negligence of many prominent organizations."[46] Childhood sexual abuse is a critical problem which has effected a significant portion of society. If communities do not work to prevent child molestation, it will continue to afflict more children with sexual dysfunctions, troubled relationships, self-esteem problems, intimacy difficulties, and a myriad of other issues as they become adults.[47]

---

[40] van Dam, Carla. (2001). *Identifying Child Molesters: Preventing Child Sexual Abuse*. New York, NY: Haworth Maltreatment and Trauma Press. P. 7.
[41] van Dam, Carla. (2001). *Identifying Child Molesters: Preventing Child Sexual Abuse*. New York, NY: Haworth Maltreatment and Trauma Press. P. 60.
[42] Putnam, Frank. (1998). *Why is it so Difficult for the Epidemic of Child Abuse to be Taken Seriously?* [Transcript] David L. Chadwick Endowed Lecture, San Diego Conference on Responding to the Maltreatment of Children, January 30, 1998.
[43] Hunter, Mic. (1990). *Abused Boys: The Neglected Victims of Sexual Abuse*. New York, NY: Fawcett Books.
[44] Larson, Carol S., Terman, Donna L., Gomby, Deanna S., Quinn, Linda Sandham, and Behrman, Richard E. (1994). Sexual Abuse of Children: Recommendations and Analysis. City, State: Publisher. P. 12.
[45] Briere, John, and Elliot, Diana. (1994). Immediate and Long-Term Impacts of Child Sexual Abuse. From *The Future of Children (4)2*, a publication of the David and Lucile Packard Foundation. Retrieved on November 25, 2005, from http://www.futureofchildren.org/usr_doc/vol4no2ART2.pdf.
[46] Lanning, Charles. (2001). *Child Molesters: A Behavioral Analysis*. Washington, DC: United States Department of Justice. P. 5.
[47] Hunter, Mic. (1990). *Abused Boys: The Neglected Victims of Sexual Abuse*. New York, NY: Fawcett Books.

Imagine[48]

I magine a childhood disease that can cause dramatic mood swings, erratic behavior, and even severe conduct disorders among those exposed; a disease that breeds distrust of adults and undermines the possibility of experiencing normal sexual relationships; a disease that can have profound implications for an individual's future health by increasing the risk of problems such as substance abuse, sexually transmitted diseases, and suicidal behavior; a disease that replicates itself by causing some of its victims to expose future generations to its debilitating effects. Imagine what we, as a society, would do if such a disease existed. We would spare no expense. We would invest heavily in basic and applied research. We would devise systems to identify those affected and provide services to treat them. We would develop and broadly implement prevention campaigns to protect our children. Wouldn't we? Such a disease does exist — it's called child sexual abuse. Our response, however, has been far from the full-court press reserved for traditional diseases or health concerns of equal or even lesser magnitude. Perhaps the perception of sexual abuse as a law enforcement problem or our discomfort in confronting sexual issues contributes to our complacency. Whatever the reason, we have severely underestimated the effects of this problem on our children's health and quality of life.

---

[48] Mercy, J. A. (1999). Having New Eyes: Viewing Child Sexual Abuse as a Public Health Problem. *Sexual Abuse: A Journal of Research and Treatment*, 11(4), 317-322.

Reflections

The following questions may help your staff members deepen their understanding of issues as they relate to your program's unique needs.

- Do you have any reactions or feelings after reviewing the number of men and women who were sexually abused as children and the impact of such abuse on their lives? What are your perceptions about the extent of the problem?
- Do you know anyone who has been sexually abused? Are they male or female? What were the circumstances? Did they disclose when the abuse was taking place? What are some of the effects of the abuse?
- What does this information tell you about the rates of sexual victimization within your youth client pool?

CHAPTER 2:
The Victims of Child Molestation

Who are the victims?

"Children and adolescents, regardless of their race,
culture, or economic status, appear to be at approximately
equal risk for sexual victimization."[49]

B y their very nature, children are "ideal" victims of sexual abuse: they are taught to obey and respect adults, they need a significant amount of attention and affection, they are naturally curious about sex, their understanding of the world is not fully developed, they are easily frightened, and they are often not believed when they complain of not liking or trusting someone.[50] As such, all children are at risk of sexual abuse. However, certain demographic and personality profiles of children can mark them as being at greater risk.

---

[49] Understanding Child Sexual Abuse. (2001) American Psychological Association Online. Retrieved November 25, 2005, from http://www.apa.org/releases/sexabuse/victims.html.
[50] Lanning, Charles. (2001). Child Molesters: A Behavioral Analysis. Washington, DC: United States Department of Justice.

*"The high number of male incarcerated offenders
reporting a history of victimization casts some doubt
on the value of gender as an identifying factor."*[51]

Gender: While both boys and girls are potential victims of child sexual abuse, estimates show that girls are twice as likely to be abused as boys. As a demographic risk factor, being a girl is clearly significant. However, it is believed that the incidence of child molestation in boys is higher than represented by statistics: "Sexual activities involving boys and adults get reported less often than sexual behaviors involving adults and girls. They speculate that this is because people see sexual activities with girls as more serious and more abusive than the same activity with boys."[52] Reasons for under-reporting molestation of boys include not only boys' reduced likelihood to come forward to professionals but also parental and societal perceptions of boys. In general, boys are seen as less vulnerable than girls. Also, what our society considers to be appropriate sexual development for boys differs greatly from the perception of what is appropriate for girls. For instance, if a boy has sexual activities with an older woman, it is often perceived as a rite of passage or as a boy "getting lucky." The same is not true of a young girl who has sexual relations with an adult male. The actual estimates of sexual molestation of boys may also go under-reported because male victims feel embarrassed, are afraid of being seen as homosexual, or, more significantly, do not perceive themselves as victims. Regardless of how society perceives boys and how boys perceive themselves, the dynamics of this type of 'relationship' are imbalanced – and no child can match the sophisticated manipulation and coercion techniques of a child molester.

Age: Victimization appears to happen at any age. The NIS-4 report showed that the rates of sexual abuse for children ages 0 to 2 have increased, evidencing broad vulnerability across the age spectrum.[53] Dr. Carla van Dam cites studies pointing to the onset of abuse for most victims occurring prior to age 16, with 48% of victims being under the age of 12. Research by D. Finkelhor and L. Baron found peak vulnerability for both boys and girls at ages 7 to 13.[54] However, when thinking about the typical age of the victims, it is

[51] Daro, Deborah. (1994). Prevention of Child Sexual Abuse. P. 201. From *The Future of Children (4)2*, a publication of the David and Lucile Packard Foundation. Retrieved on November 25, 2005, from http://www.futureofchildren.org/usr_doc/vol4no2ART2.pdf.

[52] Finkelhor, David. (1984). *Child Sexual Abuse: New Theory and Research*. New York, NY: Free Press. P. 107.

[53] Sedlack, Andrea et. al. Fourth National Incidence Study of Child Abuse and Neglect (NIS-4) Report to Congress. January 2010. Retrieved on January 6, 2014 from www.acf.hhs.gov/sites/default/opre/nis4_report_congress_full

[54] Finkelhor, D., and Baron, L. (1986). High-risk children. In D. Finkelhor (Ed.), *A Sourcebook on Child Sexual Abuse* (pp. 60-88). Beverly Hills, CA: Sage.

imperative to differentiate between the age of onset for abuse versus the risk of being abused at a particular age.

Protective Factors: Perhaps the best indicators of potential victimization are related to a child's protective factors or lack thereof. In terms of environmental factors, children with less supervision and protection of adults (and thus in greater need for affection, attention, and friendship) were found to be at increased risk of child sexual abuse.[55] Parents and single mothers undergoing stressful conditions seem to be preferred targets of child molesters. Predators tend to seek and target a child whose parent is detached or unavailable. They can spot a vulnerable child in a matter of seconds. The way a child walks and talks, the connection or lack of connection with their family, and family dysfunction or preoccupation are all noticed and exploited when a molester is targeting his or her next victim. Molesters watch for children surrounded by adults who might deny, minimize, or altogether miss the child's feelings. They seek out children who lack self-confidence and who need significant care and attention. They look for children who have already been victims of abuse. Research has found that children who are victims of molestation will be victimized multiple times and often by more than just one perpetrator.[56] The investigative work of the Child Exploitation Unit of California's San Jose Police Department discovered that many child molesters "sell" lists of names with contact information of their child victims to other molesters. These lists are considered valuable since previously-victimized children are perceived to be ideal candidates: these children's "inhibitions" have already been lowered, and they have proven, through their silence, that they are unlikely to disclose the abuse. Although we have highlighted heightened vulnerability to sexual abuse for children lacking appropriate supervision and support, researchers are quick to point out that "all children, even those from 'normal' homes and 'good' families, are at risk of seduction techniques" used by child molesters.[57] All children are at risk because of their cognitive, physical, psychological, social, and sexual stage of development.

---

[55] Finkelhor, David. (1994). Current Information on the Scope and Nature of Child Sexual Abuse. From *The Future of Children (4)2*, a publication of the David and Lucile Packard Foundation. P.48. Retrieved on November 25, 2005, from http://www.futureofchildren.org/usr_doc/vol4no2ART2.pdf.
[56] Halliday, L. (1985). *Sexual abuse: Counseling issues and concerns.* Campbell River, BC: Ptarmigan Press.
[57] Lanning, Charles. (2001). *Child Molesters: A Behavioral Analysis.* Washington, DC: United States Department of Justice. P.139.

Signs of Sexual Abuse in Children[58]

It is important to understand the signs and symptoms of sexual abuse in children, not just in the instance that a volunteer is perpetrating the abuse, but also to properly support volunteers in case the child is experiencing abuse at the hands of family, extended family, friend/s, other adults, or even other children. During your regular check-in time with a volunteer or family member, you may be likely to hear them hint at issues the child is having. It's important to talk through these issues by asking questions. Rarely do mentors or family members know or say that a child is being abused. They normally give indirect hints; they have bits of information and are unsure of what to do with it. Normally they ask a question about signs or symptoms of abuse, trying to keep some distance from themselves and the possible abuse. Adults often give you only a small piece of what they know, which is really no different for children who are asking questions or trying to report that someone is hurting them. They are cautious and hesitant and know that something "bad" is likely to happen as a result of them saying outright that abuse is taking place. They test the waters for their own sense of safety to see if they will be believed, accepted, or punished in some way.

If a child is being abused by someone at home, they may fear reprisal or removal from the home. They often feel that they are responsible for what has happened to them. They may feel that if they hadn't liked the perpetrator, if they hadn't needed someone, this wouldn't have happened. They feel tremendous shame and humiliation. Male children who are abused by a male can feel that they asked for it to happen and that they are gay, not realizing that men who molest boys are doing it not because they are gay but because they are child molesters who target male children. Females being molested might feel that is the only way they can receive love and kindness. Children might believe that this is all that they deserve and are worth.

Children who are abused often share common behaviors. Any behavior alone can be a natural, normal response for a child. It is important to keep in mind

---

[58] Keele, Lorey. (2004). Redwood Community Action Agency Northcoast Mentor Program and Council. Humboldt County Rape Crisis Team, Child Assault Prevention Project. Unpublished manuscript.

that we are discussing "extreme" behavior which is consistent with a long duration of abuse. Behavioral indicators for concern include:

- Physical: unexplainable scars or bruises caused by self or others, discomfort sitting, injuries in various stages of healing, complaints of vague physical symptoms, childhood pregnancy, venereal disease, self-mutilation
- Body language: tight, apprehensive, loose, uncontrolled, extreme fidgeting, flinching, drawing back from parents or others
- Appearance: clothing covering all body parts, several layers even in the summer, or the extreme opposite
- Emotional: outbursts of emotion or no display or change of expression, timidity, extremes in behavior (extremely aggressive or withdrawn), dull or flattened affect, clingy or indiscriminate attachments, frightened of a particular person, cries when it is time to go with the mentor or home
- Sexual: inappropriate touching of self or others, exhibits too much sexual knowledge for age, focuses on sexual topics, sexual promiscuity
- Academic: extremes in academic functioning or performing, inability to concentrate or focus, disciplinary/behavioral problems in school or the opposite – tries to be invisible
- Behavior: sudden change in behavior, excessive clinging behavior, regressive behaviors or withdrawal into a fantasy world, anxiety, depression/apathetic, phobias, suicidal behavior, chronic run-away, truancy, fear of adults, recent change in appetite, sleep disorder, poor peer relationships, poor concept of self

Reflections

The following questions may help your staff members deepen their understanding of issues as they relate to your program's unique needs.

- Are there any traits, characteristics, or circumstances that could potentially place the children you serve at an elevated risk of childhood sexual abuse?
- Do you disclose to your mentors whether or not their mentee has been a victim of sexual abuse? Could this disclosure make your mentees more vulnerable?
- Does your organization have written policies in place on how to handle disclosure of sexual abuse? Are staff members trained on these policies? Have you ever had to report abuse? How was it handled?

CHAPTER 3:
The Perpetrators of Child Molestation

What Are They Thinking?

It is difficult for most individuals to comprehend and process why an adult would want to have sexual relations with a child. Perhaps the best source of information comes from the child molesters themselves. Organizations such as NAMBLA (North American Man Boy Lover Association) actively support and advocate for "consensual" sexual acts between adults and children and seek societal acceptance for their sexual attraction to children. As stated on their website, "NAMBLA's goal is to end the extreme oppression of men and boys in mutually consensual relationships by building understanding and support for such relationships; educating the general public on the benevolent nature of man/boy love." In their view, boylovers should be allowed to express their sexual attraction to children in the same way that adults can express their sexual attraction toward one another.

Although NAMBLA is perhaps one of the most well-known boylover organizations, there are many other organizations with similar goals. These include the Pedophile Information Exchange, The Wergupp Pedophile, the Norwegian Pedophile Group, The Human Face of Pedophilia, MARTJN, Amnesty for Child Sexuality, the Guyon Society, the Child Sensuality Circle, the Pedo-Alert Network, the Lewis Carrol Collector's Guild, the Diaper Pail Fraternity, the Pedophile Liberation Front, and countless other Internet newsgroups, chat rooms, and literature actively and openly promoting adult-child sex.[59][60]

---

[59] Lanning, Charles. (2001). *Child Molesters: A Behavioral Analysis*. Washington, DC: United States Department of Justice. Pp. 13, 141.
[60] van Dam, Carla. (2001). *Identifying Child Molesters: Preventing Child Sexual Abuse*. New York, NY: Haworth Maltreatment and Trauma Press. P. 135.

Many child molesters see themselves as a sexual minority and believe they are part of a liberation movement such as those led by homosexuals and feminists. As a group, they typically believe that they are more sexually open-minded, perceiving others in our society to be repressed. They see themselves as being discriminated against and believe that, through advocacy, society will come to understand their view. As explained in material provided by the Pedophile Liberation Front,

> The problem is that today ... most "real pedophiles," as you call them, do not have a voice. It's hard to be effective when you have to remain anonymous. If we were heroes, we would come out one by one and show the world how we are not worse people than any other category, and that in fact we often care more about the child's welfare than its own parents - only we have a different idea of its welfare. But we are not heroes, so it will take more time. Put up more and more sites like this one, and some people at least will see things in a different way than is portrayed by the media ... people who hate pedophiles don't really love children. They don't give a damn about children, they want to hate us. Because we are different - and all @#$%% need someone different to hate, be it Jews, pedophiles or Blacks.[61]

Child molesters rationalize their behavior in many ways. They convince themselves that the child enjoys sexual contact or that the sexual contact is an expression of love. They rationalize their behavior by looking only at the "benefits" their relationship provides the child: attention, love, gifts, and friendship. They perceive their actions as being acceptable to the child because they rarely use violence or physical force. They believe that children are sexual beings, and they want to teach or guide them in developing their identity in an effort to rationalize their behavior.

Child molesters tend to be highly or overly sexualized adults or teens who are often fixated on particular characteristics (age, gender, look, or body type) of a child, much the same way an adult male is attracted to tall blondes or petite brunettes. In the mind of a perpetrator, all touching and interactions with their child victims are considered sexual contact. They view their interactions with children as flirtatious or suggestive, much like adults view their interactions with other adults in whom they have a sexual interest. Smiling, having a good time, hugging, or sitting on the perpetrator's lap are all perceived as sexually-suggestive actions, allowing perpetrators to transfer blame onto the child.

---

[61] Pedophile Liberation Front. Retrieved November 27, 2005, from
http://www.alicepix.com/gla/plf/fft/interview.html. Note: this website address frequently changes.

Information found on a portion of www.boylinks.net holds particular relevance to youth-serving organizations. This site encourages "boylovers" to become involved in organizations which serve children – although readers are then quickly advised that the community service opportunities listed are not intended to facilitate inappropriate contact with boys. The Community Involvement page reads, "BoyLinks includes information about community involvement as a service to responsible individuals sincerely looking for ways to help others. Organizations that serve children have stringent screening procedures, including extensive background checks. By linking to these sites, Free Spirits does not imply that boylovers ought to use them to facilitate inappropriate contact with boys. No such intent is intended or should be inferred."[62] This message is then followed by direct links to youth serving organizations such as mentoring groups, adoption agencies, and foster youth parenting programs. Other pages found on the website include discussion boards, resources for boylovers, and boys in literature, movies, music, and the arts.

Organizations such as BoyLinks support individuals who believe that there is nothing wrong with adult-child sex and that children have the capacity to and should be encouraged to make their own decisions about sex. To better understand the viewpoint of such organizations and their members, it is useful to view their own statements. Here is an excerpt of the Pedophile Liberation Front Manifesto:[63]

"The Pedo-Lib Manifesto is an attempt to affirm the right to existence of the pedophiles' sexuality and feelings. I wrote this because I am sick and tired of what I read in the papers every day. "Pedophile" has become an insult. Pedophiles are the least understood category on earth ... I want to be free. I WANT to be able to express my sexuality freely. I want to meet and consort with people who share it, and I do not want to be discriminated for it in any way. I don't want to be called "rapist," "pervert," or "criminal." I am none of those ... I BELIEVE that through a better understanding of it, people will be less frightened and will see it in a more proper light ... I WANT to be allowed to meet children although I may be known as a pedophile, in the same way as an heterosexual male is allowed to meet adult females (and vice-versa) ... I REALIZE that society thinks that having sex is unhealthy for a child, even more so with an adult. This is not true, but it is the general view ... Now hear me I WILL continue to affirm the legitimacy of my

---

[62] BoyLinks. Retrieved November 27, 2005, from
http://www.boylinks.net/resources_communityinvolvement.html.
[63] Pedophile Liberation Front. Pedo-Lib Manifesto. Retrieved November 25, 2005, from
http://www.alicepix.com/gla/plf/fft/pedo_lib_i.html. Note: this website address frequently changes.

sexuality at all times, through all means, and to anyone. I WILL continue to meet with the friends that share my desires and views; to exchange with them thoughts, experiences, and pictures; to see, talk, and smile to children, especially the ones I like; to fight all attempts to condemn me for my thoughts and actions. I WILL NOT BE SILENCED. I WILL NOT BE SUBDUED."

Such organizations are allowed to express and promote their views through websites, literature, and even annual conferences. They are protected through our Nation's Freedom of Speech. Likewise, as individuals and organizations that serve youth, we should exercise our own freedom of speech by becoming better informed, sharing information, and properly training our staff members, as well as carefully screening and monitoring our volunteers to protect children from individuals and groups seeking "consensual" sex with children.

Typology: Molesters and their Relationship to the Victim

"The molester does not lurk in dark alleys,
but lives in the child's home and is included in the child's social network."[64]

It is commonly known that the majority of child molestation takes place at the hands of individuals who are known to the victims. In fact, approximately 90% of all childhood sexual abuse is perpetrated by someone that children and their families know and trust.[65][66] One common way to classify or categorize child molesters is based on their relationship to the child. Childhood sexual abuse can be broken down into stranger abuse, family abuse, and non-family abuse.

Stranger Sexual Abuse: The stranger as the perpetrator of abuse is believed by our society to be the most common forms of abuse. In actuality, stranger sexual abuse makes up a very small portion of sexual abuse.

---

[64] van Dam, Carla. (2001). *Identifying Child Molesters: Preventing Child Sexual Abuse.* New York, NY: Haworth Maltreatment and Trauma Press.
[65] Abel, Gene G. and Harlow, Nora. (2001). *The Stop Child Molestation Book: What Ordinary People Can Do In Their Everyday Lives to Save Three Million Children.* Philadelphia, PA: Xlibris.
[66] Finkelhor, David. (1994). Current Information on the Scope and Nature of Child Sexual Abuse. From *The Future of Children (4)2,* a publication of the David and Lucile Packard Foundation. P.45. Retrieved on November 25, 2005, from http://www.futureofchildren.org/usr_doc/vol4no2ART2.pdf.

Family Sexual Abuse: Also known as incest or interfamilial sexual abuse, family abuse is perpetrated by a relative or family member, such as a father, mother, stepfather, stepmother, grandparent, brother, sister, uncle, aunt, or cousin.[67] Estimates point to family abuse as being the most common type of abuse. However, researchers point out that the rates of family abuse may appear higher than other forms since many child sexual abuse estimates are derived from Child Protective Services which has a specific emphasis on safety within the home.

Non-Family Sexual Abuse: Acquaintance or non-family sexual abuse is difficult to prevent and recognize because it involves people whom the victims and their families know and trust: "How do you warn children about pedophiles who may be their teachers, coaches, clergy members, or neighbors and whose only distinguishing characteristics are that they will treat children better than most adults, listen to their problems and concerns, and fill their emotional and physical needs?"[68] Fortunately, youth-serving organizations can make a significant impact in preventing non-family sexual abuse by preventing child molesters from gaining access to youth.

Gene Abel and Nora Harlow analyzed the reports of 4,007 adults (ages 18 to 95) who admitted that they had molested one or more children.[69] They found that only 10% molested children they did not know. Approximately 68% of child molesters sexually abused children in their own families (i.e., nieces, nephews, grandchildren). Forty percent (40%) molested children within their social circle whom they knew and with whom they associated on a regular basis. Similarly, in her study of 1,000 subjects, Linda Halliday found that 57% of sexual abuse was committed by family members, while 28% was committed by friends or acquaintances.[70] Most researchers conclude, however, that child molesters cannot be classified into neat categories. Molesters will typically victimize children both within their families *and* those encountered through their social circles. These child predators will sexually abuse children to whom they have access and will rarely abuse children they do not know.

---

[67] Lanning, Charles. (2001). *Child Molesters: A Behavioral Analysis*. Washington, DC: United States Department of Justice. P. 4.
[68] Lanning, Charles. (2001). *Child Molesters: A Behavioral Analysis*. Washington, DC: United States Department of Justice. P. 5.
[69] Abel, Gene G. and Harlow, Nora. (2001). *The Stop Child Molestation Book: What Ordinary People Can Do In Their Everyday Lives to Save Three Million Children*. Philadelphia, PA: Xlibris.
[70] Halliday, L. (1985). Sexual abuse: Counselling issues and concerns. Campbell River, BC: Ptarmigan Press.

A Demographic Profile?

Over the years, multiple attempts have been made to develop a useable profile of child molesters. Studies have analyzed socio-economic status, race, age, education, background, and a variety of other factors. Unfortunately, no single demographic profile has been determined by these studies.[71][72] Gene Abel and Nora Harlow's Stop Child Molestation Study pointed to a very interesting finding: child molesters match the U.S. population in education, percentage of individuals married or formerly married, ethnicity, and religious observance.[73] For instance, they found that 46% of molesters attended college, just as 49% of Americans attended college, according to the U.S. Census. Similarly, 93% of child molesters consider themselves to be religious, as do 93% of the general population of Americans. There are, however, some important findings about the demographics of child molesters according to gender, age, sexual orientation, and history of abuse.

Gender

Most researchers have found drastic differences between the number of men and women who molest. An estimated 1 in 20 teenage boys and adult men sexually molest children, and an estimated 1 teenage girl or adult woman in every 3,300 females molests children.[74] Other researchers estimate that between 1% to 10% of abusers are women.[75][76] While it is generally believed that the vast majority of child molesters are male, it is also believed that there are greater number of female offenders than the research seems to indicate. Reasons for under-reporting women as offenders include society's perception of women as caretakers, as non-violent, and often as less sexual than men. As stated by one clinician, "When I first began working in a mental health clinic, I would contact child protection workers as required by law when I suspected child abuse in a family. After several cases, I began to notice a disturbing pattern. When I reported a case that

---

[71] Salter, A. (1995). *Transforming trauma: A guide to understanding and treating adult survivors of child sexual abuse*. Newbury Park, CA: Sage.

[72] Groth, A.N., Hobson, W., and Gary, T. (1982). *The child molester: Clinical observations. In Social Work and Child Sexual Abuse*, (pp. 129-144). New York, NY: Haworth Press.

[73] Abel, Gene G. and Harlow, Nora. (2001). *The Stop Child Molestation Book: What Ordinary People Can Do In Their Everyday Lives to Save Three Million Children*. Philadelphia, PA: Xlibris.

[74] Abel, Gene G. and Harlow, Nora. (2001). *The Stop Child Molestation Book: What Ordinary People Can Do In Their Everyday Lives to Save Three Million Children*. Philadelphia, PA: Xlibris. P. 23.

[75] Finkelhor. David. (1994). Current Information on the Scope and Nature of Child Sexual Abuse. From *The Future of Children (4)2*, a publication of the David and Lucile Packard Foundation. P.46. Retrieved on November 25, 2005, from http://www.futureofchildren.org/usr_doc/vol4no2ART2.pdf.

[76] Abel, Gene G. and Harlow, Nora. (2001). *The Stop Child Molestation Book: What Ordinary People Can Do In Their Everyday Lives to Save Three Million Children*. Philadelphia, PA: Xlibris.

involved a girl or a boy being abused by an adult male, there was rapid and efficient action. However, when I reported a boy being abused by an adult female, very little was done; in many cases nothing was done." [77]

In his book *Abused Boys*, Mic Hunter cites a study in which 521 parents were asked to rate the seriousness of sexual abuse committed by men and women. The study concluded that subjects were more likely to see the sexual abuse as less serious when the perpetrators were women. Hunter goes on to point out that in cases where both parents were charged with child abuse, treatment providers were more likely to see the women as victims being forced to do the abuse by the men in their lives, rather than as co-perpetrators. Therefore, while estimates seem to indicate that the majority of sexual abuse perpetrators are men, we cannot automatically assume safety when working with female volunteers.

Age

"Although most identified offenders are adults,
this only reflects the point at which their behavior is recognized as an offense,
not the onset of their sexual pathology."[78]

Most individuals in our society still believe that only older men sexually abuse children – the image of the "dirty old man" clouds our judgment once more. In their study of child molestation, Abel and Harlow found that child molesters develop a sexual attraction for children early in life. They found that more than 40% of molesters sexually abuse children before they reach the age of 15, and the majority will do so before they turn 20. Judith Becker, in her research on the characteristics of offenders, cites several studies showing that between 58% to 80% of offenders admit to the onset of sexual abuse as teenagers. She also found that approximately 90% of youth sex offenders molested children they knew.[79] Pedophilia starts early. Many perpetrators begin trying to gain access to youth through babysitting or volunteering. As stated by a convicted molester, "At fourteen, I decided to join the Boy Scouts. By joining scouting at fourteen, I made what I believe was my first conscious decision to participate in an activity solely for the

[77] Hunter, Mic. (1990). *Abused Boys: The Neglected Victims of Sexual Abuse*. Toronto, Canada: The Ballantine Publishing Group. P. 37.

[78] Groth, A.N., Hobson, W., & Gary, T. (1982). *The child molester: Clinical observations. In Social Work and Child Sexual Abuse,* (pp. 129-144). New York, NY: Haworth Press.

[79] Becker, Judith. (1994). Offenders: characteristics and treatment. From *The Future of Children (4)2*, a publication of the David and Lucile Packard Foundation.

potential victims that it offered me ... I was at an age when continuing to associate with boys who were significantly younger than myself was bound to draw undue attention and unwanted suspicion ... I needed to find safe ways of being around ten- and eleven-year-olds."[80] Understanding the sexual attractions of younger children has very interesting implications for the youth-serving field. First, it points to the necessity of properly screening juvenile volunteers. Most importantly, it highlights the importance of identifying and providing appropriate intervention services for children who may be developing a sexual interest in younger children.

---

[80] Hammel-Zabin, Amy. (2003). *Conversations with a Pedophile: In the Interest of Our Children.* Fort Lee, NJ: Barricade Books, Inc. P. 48.

When the Molester is a Young Person: A Checklist to Help Parents, Teachers, and Counselors Identify Children with a Possible Sex-Specific Problem[81]

- Any child using sexual language beyond his or her age group. This suggests that the child has been looking at sexual material or engaging in sexual behavior beyond his or her age group.
- Any child who acts out sexually at school.
- Any child who continues to engage in chronic sexually harassing behavior after an adult has told the child to stop.
- Any child who others report as having excessively sexually provocative behavior.
- Any child attempting to get another child or adult nude, especially at school or outside of the home.
- Any child who is overly attentive to younger children (three or more years younger).
- Any child suspected of having a sexually transmitted disease.

If any child or teenager you know falls under any of these categories, that child may be developing an inappropriate sexual interest in other, younger children and/or may have been sexually molested themselves. As an adult hero, there are actions you can take. A child exhibiting this type of behavior needs an evaluation by a sex-specific therapist to determine the cause of the behavior. That therapist can provide a treatment plan to stop the developing inappropriate sexual interest in its tracks and/or can refer a victimized child to a therapist who specializes in child victims of sexual abuse. Sometimes both types of treatment are necessary.

It is an unfortunate fact that some children who are molested also develop their own inappropriate sexual interest in other, younger children (because of the molestation and through no fault of their own) and are at risk to become future abusers without a professional intervention. The greater the number of

[81] Abel, Gene G. and Harlow, Nora. (2001). *The Stop Child Molestation Book: What Ordinary People Can Do In Their Everyday Lives to Save Three Million Children.* Philadelphia, PA: Xlibris.

molestation incidents, the greater the chance that the molested child may develop an inappropriate sexual interest in other, younger children. It is also possible for children who have never been molested to develop an inappropriate sexual interest in other, younger children (also through no fault of their own). In either case, professional help from a sex-specific therapist is necessary.

Sex-specific therapists and therapists who specialize in child victims of sexual abuse are two very different types of therapists and each should be consulted for each separate problem. Most therapists who specialize in the treatment of molestation victims do not have the specialized training or tools to effectively treat a child's or teenager's developing inappropriate sexual interest in other, younger children. To find a qualified sex-specific therapist, please refer to "Six Questions to Ask When Selecting A Sex-Specific Therapist" and "Sex-Specific Therapy Sites in North America" on www.childmolestationprevention.org.

Sexual Orientation

Most researchers seem to agree that "despite a common myth, homosexual men are not more likely to sexually abuse children than heterosexual men are."[82] Abel and Harlow's child molestation study found that out of the 1,038 men who molested boys, more than 70% described themselves as heterosexual in their adult sexual preferences. Nine percent (9%) described themselves as equally heterosexual and homosexual, and only 8% reported being exclusively homosexual. It is important to note that child molestation is an issue of adults who are primarily sexually attracted to children. It is a situation involving manipulation, power, control, and coercion where a child is seduced into sexual activities. It is not an issue of adults who are sexually attracted to other adults – regardless of the gender to which they are primarily attracted.[83]

Interestingly, Abel and Harlow also found that 77% of admitted child molesters were married, again closely matching the 73% of all Americans who are married. It is critical to realize that although pedophiles prefer to engage in sexual activities with children, they often also have sexual relations with adults. Some of those relationships are used as a "cover." Other molesters will purposely marry women with children of their specific age preference in order to have opportunities to molest them. [84]

---

[82] Understanding Child Sexual Abuse. (2001) American Psychological Association Online. Retrieved 2004 from http://www.apa.org/releases/sexabuse/perpetrators.html

[83] Groth, A.N., and Gary, T.S. (1982). *Heterosexuality, homosexuality, and pedophilia: Sexual offenses against children and adult sexual orientation*. In A.M. Scacco (Ed.), Male Rape: A Casebook of Sexual Aggressions (pp. 143-152). New York, NY: AMS Press.

[84] Lanning, Charles. (2001). *Child Molesters: A Behavioral Analysis*. Washington, DC: United States Department of Justice. P. 17.

Past History of Abuse

"Just as the battered child runs a high risk of becoming a battering parent,
so too, does the sexually victimized child – especially the male –
run a high risk of becoming a sexual victimizer."[85]

In discussing this topic, it is critical that we do not again victimize abuse victims by assuming that they are all are child molesters. Most researchers agree that while the great majority of victims of child abuse do not become child molesters, the majority of child molesters were at one point sexually abused.

So, what conclusions can be made from these studies about a demographic profile? The majority of molesters are men, although there is still debate about the actual number of female offenders. Rarely do they molest complete strangers: child molesters abuse children to whom they have access. Child molesters can be married or single, educated or uneducated, rich or poor, young or old, and from any ethnic group. No assumptions of safety can be made by simply recruiting volunteers from high socio-economic or social status within the community. Just because someone is educated, well-employed, or a long-time respected member of the community, they should not be considered safe without further investigation. Lacking knowledge and awareness, many organizations believe that teachers, police officers, board members, or service group leaders do not need to be screened because they are known, upstanding members of the community. The mentality that child molesters are one of "them" is exactly how children are put at risk, with research demonstrating that any one of "us" could be a child predator.

Research into the demographic profiles of child molesters has proven more useful in ruling out such a profile than they have been in discovering one. However, these studies were in no way in vain since they help to establish two critical findings. First, many myths surrounding the "typical" molester have been debunked. Second, this research has pointed toward a profile not based on physical characteristics but on repeated and, to some extent, identifiable actions. Current research into child molester profiles focus more on this "action profile" than on any demographic one.[86]

---

[85] Groth, A.N., Hobson, W., and Gary, T. (1982). *The child molester: Clinical observations. In Social Work and Child Sexual Abuse,* (pp. 129-144). New York, NY: Haworth Press.

[86] van Dam, Carla. (2001). *Identifying Child Molesters: Preventing Child Sexual Abuse.* New York, NY: Haworth Maltreatment and Trauma Press.

Interview with Whitney Gabriel, National Director, Child Safety, Abel Screening, Inc.[87]

Q. How bad is the problem?

A. We estimate that currently in this country 3 million children are victims of child sexual abuse. To break that number down into something a little more understandable, in an average eighth grade class of 30 children, we can expect that 4 girls have already been molested, 2 boys have already been molested, and that there is 1 boy who has already molested a younger child. Thus, child sexual abuse is a very significant problem in this country and adults should learn everything they can about how to prevent it.

Q. What percentage of child molestation comes from family members, friends/acquaintances, or strangers? We are obviously most interested in the friend/acquaintance category as this is the area that pertains to volunteer agencies.

A. According to the Abel and Harlow Child Molestation Prevention Study, of the 4,000 admitted molesters studied, 68% targeted children in their own families, 40% targeted children of friends and child acquaintances, and 10% targeted children who are strangers. (Note that because sexual abusers often molest children in more than one category, the categories total more than 100%.)

Q. Should organizations working with children 14 years of age or older be as concerned about child molestation?

A. Yes, children 14 years of age or older are at risk of being molested. The people who abuse them are called "ephebophiles." Ephebophiles are people who have a sexual interest in children who are post-pubescent.

---

[87] Gabriel, Whitney. Formerly with Child Molestation Research and Prevention Institute (personal correspondence, 2004).

Q. Across the nation there are now many mentoring programs which utilize youth as their volunteer mentors. As an example, they may "match" or pair together elementary school children with high school students. What percentage of child molestation involves youth as the molesters? Should these organizations be as concerned about potential child molestation?

A. Yes, organizations should be equally concerned about preventing molestation in their programs that involve pairing up older or teenaged children with younger children. According to the Abel and Harlow Child Molestation Prevention Study, of the 4,000 admitted sexual abusers that they studied, 20% reported that they had their first victim before they were 10 years old, another 43% began to molest between the ages of 10 and 15, and a total of 76% said they had their first child victim before they were 20 years old. Organizations should be aware of this and take precautions when pairing up older children and teenagers with younger children, just as they do when matching up adults with children.

Q. What about site-based programs, where mentors and mentees meet only in supervised conditions? Should they be as concerned about potential child molestation?

A. Organizations must keep in mind that abusers who have a sexual interest in children will try to manipulate or convince the child or the child's family to allow for unsupervised time with the child outside of the organization's formal setting. Despite setting strict rules, organizations cannot guarantee that unsupervised time will not occur. Thus, site-based programs should also screen and take other safety precautions with volunteers who will work with children.

Q. Do you have any other thoughts about volunteer screening?

A. One of our concerns is that while many organizations rely on criminal background checks as a screening tool, these checks alone may give organizations and parents a false sense of security that if a volunteer has passed a criminal background check, the person is safe to work with children. It is important to understand that the vast, vast majority of child sexual abuse cases never get reported to the authorities and thus criminal background checks are only effective at screening out the smallest minority of abusers from working with children. Criminal background checks are a useful tool, but it is important to recognize that the protection they offer is quite limited.

Reflections

The following questions may help your staff members deepen their understanding of issues as they relate to your program's unique needs.

- What images, ideas, and feelings come to mind when you think of a child molester?
- What are your feelings or reactions in response to learning that there are organizations that actively promote and try to legitimatize adult-child sex?
- Who makes up your volunteer pool? Could you imagine any of your current volunteers as potential child molesters?
- Are staff members in your organization trained to recognize and provide appropriate support/referral for children who may be developing pedophilia?

CHAPTER 4:
The Dynamics of the Abuse

"Sometimes a violent act is so frightening that we call the perpetrator a monster, but as you'll see, it is by finding his humanness - his similarity to you and me – that such an act can be predicted."[88]

Child molesters cannot be identified by merely looking at their traits and characteristics. They are diverse in their socio-economic background, level of education, religious preference, ethnic heritage, and age. How, then, can youth-serving agencies identify child molesters and prevent their access to children? The answer lies in the dynamics of the abuse and the behavioral patterns of child molesters. Much of this information has been collected from the molesters themselves, as they share information on how and why they have molested children. Child predators with a sexual interest in children gain access to youth, seducing them over time into sexual abuse. This process can be categorized into four components or preconditions for sexual abuse:[89]

- An individual becomes aware of, fantasizes about, and justifies their sexual interest in children.
- An individual identifies a vulnerable child or organization through which he or she can gain access to children.

---

[88] de Becker, Gavin. (1997). *The Gift of Fear*. New York, NY: Dell Publishing. P.15.
[89] The foundation of this model relies principally on the theoretical framework of David Finkelhor, modified by research drawn from Dr. Nick A. Groth, Dr. Carla van Dam's Identifying Child Molesters, Charles Lanning's Child Molesters: A Behavioral Analysis, and the Child Sexual Exploitation Unit of the San José Police Department.

- The perpetrator overcomes obstacles to abuse by becoming known to and trusted by the community, as well as the family and/or members of the youth organization.
- The perpetrator seduces, isolates, lowers the inhibitions of, and abuses a victim. By understanding these stages and their complexities, we can learn how to effectively screen and monitor volunteers to prevent child sexual abuse.

Awareness, Fantasy, and Justification of Interest

Generally, child molesters will go through their own internal process prior to abusing a child.[90] First, they will become aware of their sexual interest in children. For the majority of child molesters, this awareness of their sexual feelings for children develops at a young age. As adolescents, they may notice themselves becoming aroused by children significantly younger than they are. They will then begin to develop recurrent and elaborate fantasies about engaging in sexual relations with younger children. They will seek to nurture these feelings by collecting child pornography, seeking publications that support their sexual beliefs and practices, or even talking to other molesters. They will begin to rationalize their interest in children by denying that their behavior could cause children any harm, viewing the children as willing participants, emphasizing the benefits the relationship will bring to the child, and even condemning adults for shaming and repressing the sexual needs of children.[91] Once these individuals rationalize their behavior and lower their own internal inhibitions to abuse, they will then identify and try to gain access to vulnerable children.

Identifying a Vulnerable Child

"A percentage of predators will target child-service groups because they provide access to samples of highly vulnerable children and often there are opportunities for isolated access.
Many of these children have already been molested, making them more vulnerable to the predator."[92]

[90] San Jose Police Department Child Exploitation Unit. (2002). Child Sexual Exploitation Training CD.
[91] van Dam, Carla. (2001). *Identifying Child Molesters: Preventing Child Sexual Abuse.* New York, NY: Haworth Maltreatment and Trauma Press. Pp. 92-93.
[92] Sirota, Perry. Sirota Psychological Services, Calgary, Alberta (personal communication 2004).

Individuals who are sexually attracted to children will seek as many opportunities as possible to feed their sexual desires and gain access to children. While some individuals believe that the primary motivator for abuse is sexual gratification, this is a very limited and inaccurate view of molestation. For the majority of molesters, the primary motivator is the need to control and have power over their victims. Child molesters will have recurrent and elaborate fantasies through which they map out every detail of the abuse: where it will take place, what will happen, how it will happen, and what they will say or do. Coercing a child into playing out this fantasy gives the molester a sense of power and control. The real gratification is not in the sexual act but in the process leading to the act. Their fantasies can become so elaborate that they often follow a script, including the characteristics of the children to whom they are attracted. For example, they may seek a 12- or 13-year-old boy with dark hair and dark skin, although they may settle for another child who is available. Since their plan involves coercion and manipulation, they will look for children who are vulnerable, who need love and attention, and with whom they can develop a strong bond. They will look for children with no father figure or male role model. They look for children who have had a lifetime of struggle, with a parent barely able to meet her own needs, let alone those of the child. They will look for a child who does not have a strong sense of his or her own boundaries or who struggles socially. Additionally, they will target children from families who seem stressed, are too busy, are eager for assistance, or which may be having difficulties getting along with the child. Child molesters are patient and may at times "assess" the vulnerability of multiple victims simultaneously. Once they have identified a vulnerable child from a vulnerable adult community, they will begin the grooming process.

Grooming the Community

Child molesters realize that gaining the trust of the adult community is key to having unrestricted access to children. They will "groom" or seduce adults by appearing to be nice, kind, generous individuals with a sincere interest in helping children and their families. They portray themselves as likeable and exceptionally charming. Charm, when used in this sense, is not a positive characteristic. As Gavin de Becker states in his book *The Gift of Fear*, it is important to think of charm as a verb: it has a motive, and the motive is to control by attraction.[93] Child molesters will portray whatever image and personality

---

[93] de Becker, Gavin. (1997). *The Gift of Fear*. New York, NY: Dell Publishing.

traits that will make them likeable and trusted by the community. This "chameleon-like" charm allows discrepancies to be ignored or "glossed over" and is used to successfully convince the adult community to ignore unsettling facts, suspend disbelief, and provide unimpeded access to children."[94] Organizations should scrutinize individuals who seem too good to be true.

Child molesters will constantly seek to help the adults in charge of protecting children, while asking "nothing" in return. They may often appear to be upstanding individuals with impressive track records of helping the community. However, a closer look into their helping patterns will point to consistent and extreme participation in activities involving children who fit the characteristics of the children to whom they are most attracted. For instance, they may teach middle school students, volunteer to organize an after-school play, teach bible study to children, serve as a foster parent, and then approach an organization to volunteer as a mentor. It is important to remember that not every concerned individual involved in helping youth is suspect. Over-involvement with children is just one of many red flags to be considered in screening volunteers.

It is not uncommon to encounter resistance from the adult community when they hear complaints or child molestation charges against a perpetrator. Many will be shocked and often dismiss such allegations. This occurs because they expect child molesters to be monsters but are instead confronted with someone they know, associate with, and trust. In cases of molestation, the adult community will often be quick to affirm that, "That's impossible: he is married and has children." or "It couldn't be her. She is so nice and kind." The truth of the matter is that many cases are not so unimaginable and the community would have noticed that something was not quite right if they had only observed the perpetrator's behavior and learned to recognize indicators which would have alerted them to danger.

The grooming process does not happen overnight. Perpetrators will wait until the time is right. They will likely target vulnerable families. They will offer a listening ear and a helping hand. They will make themselves indispensable. In the case of volunteer organizations, this behavior might present itself in the form of a volunteer who has become overly-involved in the life of a family. For example, they may help the family pay for rent, spend a significant amount of time associating with the family, or assume responsibilities that staff had warned volunteers not to take on during the orientation and training process.

---

[94] van Dam, Carla. (2001). Identifying Child Molesters: Preventing Child Sexual Abuse. New York, NY: Haworth Maltreatment and Trauma Press. P. 167.

A volunteer may "groom" an entire family to the point where the family is willing to violate an organization's non-negotiable rules, even after staff have insisted that the rules must not be broken. For instance, a program's "no overnights" rule might be ignored by a family when they agree to allow the volunteer to take their son on a trip. Or a program might clearly state that volunteers and children can only meet on-site while supervised; this rule may be overridden by a parent who allows the volunteer to meet in a different setting and under different conditions. While oftentimes volunteers do cross boundaries without ill intent, it is critical that organizations pay attention when this happens and assess how a volunteer responds once confronted. While most well-intentioned volunteers will correct their mistake and follow the regulations set forth by an organization, many molesters will deliberately violate boundaries to "test the waters" and see how far they can stretch the rules. Volunteers may even make the same request to several different staff members within an organization in order to see who is more agreeable or easier to manipulate. It is important that all staff members within an organization are clear about and agree upon program boundaries, policies, and procedures while maintaining ongoing communication about their volunteers.

Grooming Children

"The child predator targets potential victims the same way a marketing expert looks to tap into consumer patterns and makes well-planned strategic moves."[95]

While the child molester is grooming the adult community, he or she will also groom their target. This grooming takes place by seducing the child, slowly lowering inhibitions, isolating the child, and coercing him or her to believe that they are responsible for the abuse. The relationship between child molesters and victims holds similarities to adult/adult sexual relationships. This is not surprising, as child molesters see themselves as engaging in "consensual" sexual relationships with children. Their behavior, however, is coercive, pre-planned, and manipulative. The development and growth of the relationship does not happen by accident. Child molesters are not motivated by sexual fulfillment. Rather, they are driven by the need to control, manipulate, "play the game," and win. They want to seduce, control, abuse, and "get away with it." They get their "fix" by manipulating their victims to do what they want, and they test to see what they can make their victims do. It makes them feel powerful to take advantage of the powerless. They enjoy the thrill of the hunt.

---

[95] Sirota, Perry. Sirota Psychological Services, Calgary, Alberta (personal communication 2004).

One of the first questions most people ask is, "Why don't kids tell?" or "Why don't they just say 'No'?" The grooming process develops over time, slowly taking away the victim's power. It rarely happens as most people imagine. A child molester will not begin the abuse by forcing a child into sexual acts right away. The process is much more carefully planned. Thankfully, we can prevent and detect abuse because "although pedophiles vary greatly, their sexual behavior is repetitive and highly predictable."[96] Some of their behaviors might seem quite innocent. In fact, many child predator behaviors may be those exhibited by appropriate volunteers, and no single behavior should be considered an automatic sign of abuse. Rather, it is by understanding patterns that staff can create informed judgments.

A Close Relationship

The process of seduction begins by developing a close personal relationship with the victim. Child molesters will accomplish this by being empathetic, listening, giving positive encouragement, identifying what they need, and fulfilling their needs.[97] Child molesters feel that they treat their victim better than the other adults in the child's life. They offer all the attention and love that they need and, at least temporarily, respond to those needs. So, what is wrong with taking care of a child's need? The problem lies in intent. All of their behaviors are geared toward one purpose: to gain the trust of the child in order to abuse. Child molesters are skilled at identifying and responding to the needs and wants of their victims. They will seek to seduce or control their victims by giving them attention, affection, time, and gifts.

Abuse rarely begins right away. The perpetrator knows that they must first gain the child's trust in order to ensure their victim does not tell anyone about the abuse. As explained by one molester, "By listening to a boy, sharing secrets, and encouraging him to talk about everything that was on his mind, he usually wanted to spend time with me and inadvertently provided me with all I needed to know about his personal vulnerabilities to victimize him."[98] In order to gain the child's affection, molesters may also buy expensive gifts or treat the child to things they want. By fulfilling the child's needs in ways many adults have not, the psychological relationship and dependency on the perpetrator begins to take root.

---

[96] Lanning, Charles. (2001). *Child Molesters: A Behavioral Analysis*. Washington, DC: United States Department of Justice. P. 37.

[97] Lanning, Charles. (2001). *Child Molesters: A Behavioral Analysis*. Washington, DC: United States Department of Justice. P. 55.

[98] Hammel-Zabin, Amy. (2003). *Conversations with a Pedophile: In the interest of our children*. Fort Lee, NJ: Barricade Books, Inc. P. 118.

Perpetrators are cunning and instinctual: they see a child as prey and wait to take the child off guard or by surprise. They are able to identify a child's needs and vulnerabilities. They will try to fill whatever void they perceive the child to have in his life: an absent father, an affectionate friend, or an understanding caretaker. Ironically, the molester often becomes the most stable and connected parent figure the child has ever had. Child molesters will only provide this level of attention to their victims as long as they are interested in them and as long as their victims respond to their advances. Sadly, many children end up feeling rejected and disappointed when their molesters lose interest and move on to their next victim.

Secrecy

As a tactic to build intimacy, test the child, and later make the child believe he is a willing participant, child molesters will begin by sharing small "innocent" secrets with the child. They may buy the child something they are not supposed to have or take them to a favorite activity when they are not supposed to go: "I would test the boy in some simple fashion to see if he had the ability to keep a secret … I would, for example, swear in front of him … In this initial step I wanted the boy to see keeping of secrets as just something that we did … I would make sure that he felt trusted and 'grownup' because this adult was dealing with him on a different level."[99]

Peer-like behavior

As the relationship develops, the perpetrators will act on the same level as the child. This behavior is done partly because the perpetrators deceive themselves into thinking that they are developing a relationship between equals. This behavior is also used to convince the child that he or she is choosing or consenting to engage in the sexual acts. Child molesters will often describe their behavior as being on the same "wavelength" as the child."[100] This peer-like behavior will take many forms:[101]
• Inability to set boundaries,
• Treating the child as an adult,

---

[99] Hammel-Zabin, Amy. (2003). *Conversations with a Pedophile: In the interest of our children*. Fort Lee, NJ: Barricade Books, Inc. P. 90.
[100] van Dam, Carla. (2001). *Identifying Child Molesters: Preventing Child Sexual Abuse*. New York, NY: Haworth Maltreatment and Trauma Press. P. 108.
[101] Lanning, Charles. (2001). *Child Molesters: A Behavioral Analysis*. Washington, DC: United States Department of Justice. P. 43.

- Offering alcohol or drugs,
- Having inappropriate self-disclosure,
- Allowing the child to become their emotional caretaker,
- Developing hobbies or interests that are appealing to children,
- Having a home that is filled with things that a child would enjoy, or
- Associating with a circle of friends who are young.

Slow Desensitization

Slow desensitization to touch and sexual topics is a key factor in understanding how the abuse takes place. Once a relationship is established, the perpetrator will slowly desensitize the child to touch and sexual topics. This process takes place so slowly that, by the time a sexual act takes place, the child feels he has agreed and consented to the abuse. Child molesters rarely have to use physical force. Before a child is abused physically, he will have been manipulated psychologically into believing that he chose to engage in sexual acts.

The process may begin, for example, with the perpetrator asking seemingly innocent questions: "Do you have a girlfriend?" "Have you two kissed?" "Have your parents talked to you about sex?" The perpetrator may later introduce the topic of sexuality. He will then move on to talk about sex under the pretext of sexual education. He may make the child feel special by congratulating him on how mature he is to be able to talk about the topic so openly. The perpetrator may then introduce pornography, first showing materials with women and men having sex and later showing adults and children having sex. Then the perpetrator will begin to desensitize the child to touch. Over time, the perpetrator will test how far they can go physically. This desensitization may begin by tickling or rough-housing. It may later continue by showing the child how different sexual acts are done.

Isolation

The child molester will seek to emotionally and physically isolate the child from his community. Emotionally, he will isolate the child by becoming indispensable. If problems arise between the victim and their family, the child molester will seek to aggravate the situation. Instead of trying to help the child get along with his family and friends, the child molester will focus on and accentuate the problem. He will also make the child feel that he is the only person who understands, who cares, and who truly listens. He may say things like, "Even if your parents don't understand you, at least I'm here for you. You can tell me everything." Physically, the molester will try to isolate the child by seeking opportunities to spend alone time. As the acts of sexual abuse take place, this feeling of isolation will be heightened through the use of threats. The perpetrator will make the child believe that no one will believe him if he tells, that he will be blamed, and that he will get in trouble. Shame may also prevent the victim from telling. As explained by one child molester, "Although the 11- or 12-year-old was totally disgusted with what he was being forced to endure, he would almost always rather submit than ever risk the moral shame of everyone finding out."[102] Finally, and perhaps most sadly, the child molester will use the child's dependency on the relationship as a tool to prevent him from telling. He may say, "If you tell, they are going to hurt me. I will go to go to jail, and my life will be ruined." The Pedophile Liberation Front website gives us a glimpse of what a child molester may tell a child:

---

[102] Hammel-Zabin, Amy. (2003). *Conversations with a Pedophile: In the interest of our children.* Fort Lee, NJ: Barricade Books, Inc. P. 129.

Letter to Children[103]

You can say no, but you can also say yes: Somebody probably told you that "You can say no." Maybe they explained what it meant: if some adult asks you to do "things," you don't have to do them. This of course does not mean your Mother telling you to wash your teeth … It means only some adults, and some things. Well, just remember one thing: if you can say no, you can also say yes. That means that if you feel like doing something, you have the right to do it. No matter what your teacher told you. Because it's right. You have the choice.

Why you shouldn't tell anything: Sometimes, friends with which you have fun ask you not to tell others about what you do together. This happens often when your friends are adults. The reason for this is simple: If people find out that you've been doing 'things' with an adult friend, they may put that person in jail and ruin his/her life. Especially if your friend is a man, or even an older boy. So your friend is afraid. At this point, you should make a choice. If you feel that this person has been nice to you, and that he does not deserve to be punished, you should help him and not tell anybody - not even your pals, about what happened. Remember, telling people is like putting your friend in jail! So before you tell anyone, ask yourself: 'Does my friend deserve to go to jail?' It may well be that he does, but please think about it first or you could regret it afterwards. Oh, and there's another thing. Do you know what happens to you when people find out? Well, you go 'in therapy.' Therapy means that you meet with someone who will try to convince you that all you did with your friend was a horrible thing, and that your friend is a horrible person. And you better say so quickly, or they will never stop. They may even give you drugs to 'calm you down.' You become a sick person. So, unless you feel really really bad about what you did with your friend, think about it very well!

But what exactly is a pedophile? A 'pedophile' is an adult that is sexually attracted to children. 'Sexually' means that this person may like to touch you, rub your body against his, be very affectionate and cuddly. He (or sometimes she) may also wish to touch your private parts, or have you touch his. In short,

---

[103] Pedophile Liberation Front. Retrieved November 27, 2005, from http://alicepix.com/gla/plf/fft/letter.html. Note this website address frequently changes.

a pedophile likes to do with children what everybody else likes to do with other adults. Sometimes, you will find that there is someone you know that makes you feel good in a way you never felt before. It's called 'pleasure.' It's something that not all children experience, and if you do, you're lucky. The person that makes you feel pleasure may be a pedophile, or it may be anybody. It can be an adult or a child, a male or a female, black or white. It doesn't matter. What matters is that you feel good. When I was a child, I never met a pedophile. But I knew about pleasure. I always wanted to touch and kiss my girl friends. I felt a sort of energy going through my body, when I smelled the skin of other girls. I felt good. So, if you have the chance to feel good, why be afraid?

Reflections

The following questions may help your staff members deepen their understanding of issues as they relate to your program's unique needs.

- Does your organization have policies and procedures in place about appropriate boundaries such as gift-giving, self-disclosure, overnights, secrecy, and working with parents?
- How can this information be presented and incorporated during volunteer orientations and trainings?
- How closely do you monitor the volunteers in your program once they have been introduced to the youth?
- Do you have strong enough relationships established with the children and guardians involved with your program so that they would be likely to come to you if they felt uncomfortable with their assigned volunteer?

Learning from Case Studies

Today, there is extensive media coverage on child sexual abuse. Unlike 20 years ago, when child sexual abuse media reporting was infrequent and relatively free of investigative details, there is an abundance of information provided today that can serve as learning for youth-serving organizations.

The Jerry Sandusky/Penn State Child Abuse Scandal is a classic case that matches up with research and evidence-based practice on this topic. Some of the principles illustrated by this and other cases include:

- Extensive history and multiple victims before legal action is taken
- Knowledge of inappropriate behavior unreported by others
- Inappropriate behavior that is reported is met with denial, inaction, cover-ups
- Grooming of victims, parents, and community
- Connection to youth-service program
- Travel and isolation of victims
- Evidence of parental intuition that something wasn't right
- Youth reports not perceived as credible
- Lack of response to youth behavioral change
- Fear, gift-giving, travel used as incentives for youth participation and silence
- Perpetrator is respected, upstanding member of the community, making it challenging to believe and move forward with allegations
- Reticence of victims to report abuse

PART II
Child Molestation Prevention: Screening and Monitoring for Effectiveness

This section of SAFE delineates strategies that youth-serving organizations can incorporate into their programs to prevent child sexual abuse. This manual is not intended to be an all-encompassing guide of every critical element and consideration in screening and monitoring volunteers. We are not, for example, reviewing the qualities found in the most effective volunteers. Rather, we are specifically presenting two key concepts that organizations can and should consider in screening and monitoring volunteers to prevent child sexual abuse: Objective Data and Informed Intuition. In reviewing this information, be mindful that a volunteer organization has the legal right to accept, reject, or terminate candidates at their discretion. Your legal counsel and Board of Directors should develop guidelines for how this is handled. It should also be clear that every candidate must undergo the same process, no matter who referred them. The volunteer application process should be thoroughly completed and documented before an individual is accepted, with a final determination that is supported and respected by all. Programs should also remember that their efforts to ensure mentee safety do not end when the match begins: even after a mentor has been introduced to his or her mentee, mentoring organizations must continue to monitor the relationship to ensure the safety of their youth participants.

CHAPTER 5:
Objective Data

S creening Applicants For Effectiveness is a dual-phase process. The first phase involves utilizing mentor screening tools to gather raw, objective data on volunteer applicants. By using these tools and adhering to the mentoring field's recommended best practices, agencies create an environment conducive to effectively determining whether or not mentor candidates will be caring, supportive, and safe. All of the information gathered during this phase will be utilized in the second phase of the mentor screening process (covered in Chapter 6). Mentoring agencies typically gather additional data related to the focus of their program and the skills, talents, or background needed for the success of their mentoring objectives. For example, a mentoring program with a focus on career development might also gather resumes from their volunteer applicants. Such additional information is important for effective service delivery. The mentor screening tools described in this chapter are focused exclusively on safety: these tools are the minimum level of screening a youth-serving organization should implement for the prevention of child molestation. To help agencies explore the needs of their own program, details on each mentor screening tool are followed by a Reflections section with sample Situations. Modified to ensure confidentiality, these Situations are based on both common and uncommon mentor applicants who have applied to Friends for Youth, Inc., and other mentoring programs. Each is offered as a starting point for reflection and discussion of situations which agencies may encounter.

Tool: Interactions

Interactions include all interactions (observed or personally experienced) between a volunteer applicant (or mentor) and program staff, agency representatives, other volunteers, or other community members.

Components:

The use of interactions as a screening tool spans the entire time period of an individual's involvement with an agency: recruitment, orientation, interview, and training, as well as time spent with their mentee after the match date. This tool includes all forms of communication and all impressions generated by an applicant or mentor. Chapter 6 will describe the ways in which interactions are used, but for the purposes of screening for child predators, several concepts are particularly important:

- Questions and Comments – What types of questions does the applicant/mentor ask? What types of comments does he or she make? Are they appropriate for the setting and the situation? Does he or she voice inappropriate, atypical, or unusual questions or comments?
- Comfort and Behavior – How comfortably does the applicant/mentor interact with his or her peers? Once matched, is the mentor's behavior with his or her mentee appropriate?
- Communication – Is the applicant/mentor able to communicate with others, including staff members or adults/youth with whom he or she is observed?
- Reaction – What type of personal reactions do staff have to the applicant/mentor? What type of observed personal reactions do other participants have to him or her?
- Timing – Does the applicant/mentor respond within an appropriate amount of time? Is he or she overly anxious or particularly slow to respond to agency communications or requests?

Process:

Every step of the screening process and post-match monitoring is an opportunity to observe the applicant or mentor. The orientation and volunteer training are useful opportunities to observe applicant-applicant interactions, but telephone conversations, e-mail correspondence, and all other interactions (or lack of interactions) can also be useful.

Principles and Protocol for Staff:

From first contact with an agency, throughout the application process, and even once a candidate has been matched, an individual's interactions are reflective of that person's motivations for program participation and ability to fulfill the role of a mentor. Staff must continue to observe all applicants and mentors, keeping their coworkers updated on interactions. While unusual or unexpected interactions may be reflective of issues, stresses, or challenges in the life of the applicant or mentor, it would be naïve to automatically assume that these communications are not important.

Reflections:

The following descriptions may help your staff members deepen their understanding of issues as they relate to your program's unique needs. They are offered as a starting point for reflection and discussion of situations your agency may encounter. These scenarios and the recommendations of your legal counsel can help you prepare for similar incidents within your program.

- **Interactions Situation 1**

    An individual begins the application process with tremendous enthusiasm and excitement. The agency's program coordinator finds his behavior somewhat overzealous and is careful to report these interactions during the weekly program staff meeting. The applicant soon becomes irritated with the pace of the procedures, particularly when he is unable to attend the next training session, which is already full. He calls to speak with the program's executive director to discuss the length of the application process.

- **Interactions Situation 2**

    During an orientation session, one of the attendees appears particularly uncomfortable. She asks appropriate questions and is friendly with the staff, but she has no interactions or eye contact with any of the other attendees. The staff member conducting the session shares his observations so that his coworkers can be particularly attentive of her behavior during the remaining application process steps.

Tool: Orientation

The orientation is a volunteer applicant's initial visit to the agency and an introduction to the program.

Components:

The various components of the orientation provide applicants with a clear picture of the program, the volunteer application process, the "personality" of the agency, and the mentoring commitment. It is also often the first point of contact for staff, so it is an important step in the screening process. The tone set during the orientation is an extremely useful self-selection tool: child predators are less likely to pursue participation in a program which clearly indicates its focus on extensive screening and ongoing monitoring. Unfortunately, some child predators will continue the applicant process. Chapter 6 will describe the ways in which orientation information is used, but for the purposes of screening for child predators, several orientation components are particularly important:

- Focus – Organizations should highlight the program's purpose, goals, focus, and beneficiaries.
- Process – Staff should present both the application and mentoring processes so that applicants understand the level of screening and ongoing monitoring.
- Screening – Each step of the application process should be described. This includes the in-home interview, character reference checks, state and federal background checks, driving record, volunteer training, and final selection process.
- Records – Staff members should clearly state that all application material is confidential and becomes the property of the agency.
- Final Decision – Programs should provide a brief statement regarding the selection and approval of volunteer applicants, as well as the way in which disqualified applicants will be notified.

Process:

The orientation should provide a professional yet welcoming setting. For appropriate mentor candidates, the orientation may encourage their participation based on the positive staff support and professional approach to youth needs. This same environment can illustrate a different image to child predators: an agency with a stringent screening process and whose staff is intimately interested in and involved with each child and mentoring relationship may not facilitate their ultimate objective. The orientation should ideally take place in the agency's facilities and cover information which is more detailed than that presented in recruitment presentations or at volunteer fairs. As applicants arrive, basic sign-in information should be gathered, such as their name, contact information, and how each applicant learned of the program. Staff should begin with an orientation agenda, then cover the program history, objectives, beneficiaries, application/screening process, program time commitment, and the roles and responsibilities of a mentor, including the program's matching protocols (e.g., ethnicity-based matches, same gender or mixed gender matches, etc.). Near the end of the orientation, staff should offer an opportunity for applicants to ask questions. The orientation should be concluded by letting candidates know that they will be contacted within a specified time frame (i.e., within a week, within the month).

Principles and Protocol for Staff:

The orientation is often the first contact point for staff and volunteer applicants, so it is important for staff to interact with and observe applicants as much as possible. Whenever possible, it is extremely useful to have two staff members present at orientation sessions: having two staff members will maximize an agency's ability to conduct the orientation while observing the volunteer applicants. This may be particularly effective for agencies conducting "open door" orientations (i.e., sessions for which no previous agency contact or RSVP is required). Through the orientation, staff can meet each candidate, observe them in a setting with their peers, ask how they heard of the organization, and ask about their motivations to mentor. The tone of the orientation is crucial. Because it is a challenge to recruit long-term mentors, agencies must balance thanking applicants for their interest with presenting the application and monitoring procedures. When describing the application steps, programs should emphasize that the process serves as part of both the agency's screening and matching process. Ultimately, the orientation should create an impression of a knowledgeable organization which is serious and thorough in its approach to screening and monitoring. Child molesters develop a keen ability to identify vulnerabilities in their youth targets and families, as well as in organizations. These candidates will be using the orientation to answer specific questions:

- What is the agency's screening process?
- What type(s) of children are served?
- Do staff members seem overwhelmed or too eager to accept volunteer applicants, particularly male applicants?
- How many staff members are dedicated to monitoring the match?
- How often do program staff contact mentors?
- Does the program keep in touch with mentees and their families?
- When will this monitoring end?

The question period toward the end of the orientation is a particularly useful opportunity to learn more about each applicant's motivations and interests. Having a second staff person present can be useful in observing the expressions and reactions of all attendees while the presenter is directing his or her attention elsewhere. The challenge of volunteer recruitment often results in program staff thanking applicants profusely for their orientation attendance, then focusing on the ease of the application process. Organizations which make this error send the wrong message to applicants, suggesting to child predators that they may encounter little scrutiny in such an organization. Instead, it is important for agencies to let both appropriate candidates and child predators know that the program's priority is the safety and well-being of children. Ideally, agencies will carefully prepare staff on what to say – or not say – during an orientation session. For example, organizations should prepare standardized responses for information that is not generally included in the orientation but is periodically asked by volunteer applicants. These types of questions include the reasons for rejection from the program or specific "mistakes" that would delay the application process. By preparing staff members to answer in a professional manner without being specific, programs can avoid providing potential molesters with the information they need to successfully navigate a program's application process. After the orientation, staff should remember that applicants who do not respond to the agency's contact after an orientation should not be pursued relentlessly. At best, these applicants may be unable to adhere to the requested mentoring time commitment, or their lack of contact may reflect an inability to make and keep commitments (which is best to uncover before a match). At worst, these applicants may be child predators who felt the screening and monitoring process would have uncovered their motivations. Excessive pursuit of these applicants could illustrate a program's desperation for mentors, a desperation which will not be lost on an applying child predator.

Reflections:

The following descriptions may help your staff members deepen their understanding of issues as they relate to your program's unique needs. They are offered as a starting point for reflection and discussion of situations your agency may encounter. These scenarios and the recommendations of your legal counsel can help you prepare for similar incidents within your program.

- **Orientation Situation 1**

  During an orientation, a male applicant asked whether he could be matched with a female mentee. The staff member explained that the program does not conduct male mentor/female mentee matches. The applicant insisted that many girls are lacking a male role model and that some girls could benefit from a male mentor. The staff member responded that her role during the orientation was to describe the services offered through the agency and that the agency only matches female mentees with female mentors. The applicant muttered his displeasure at this response. After the orientation, the staff member added her observations to the applicant's record; the record on this applicant included two telephone conversations during which he asked about being matched with a female mentee.

- **Orientation Situation 2**

  Two staff members were present for an orientation which included eight attendees. The group was talkative and enthusiastic, asking questions throughout the session. The orientation presenter provided all of the agency material, and he was careful to utilize the organization's standardized responses for questions regarding the application process, issues which may preclude a candidate from being accepted, and questions regarding an applicant's criminal and juvenile records. While the staff presenter answered these questions, the second staff member noticed that one applicant rolled his eyes and smirked during several responses. After the orientation, both staff members shared and documented their impressions of each candidate, including the specific topics which elicited the unusual responses from the applicant in question.

Tool: Background Checks

Fingerprinting is used to conduct state- and federal-level background checks related to an applicant's criminal history of indictments and convictions of child abuse, sexual offense charges, violent crimes, arson, and drug charges. The Sexual Offender Registry (or Megan's Law Database) can be used to conduct federal-level background checks related to an applicant's convictions of sexual offense charges. Additional details on both fingerprinting and Sexual Offender Registries are included in Part III of this volume.

Components:

All volunteer applicants should be screened at both the state and federal level to ensure that both local and non-local records are obtained. The process for conducting fingerprint checks varies by state. At this time, the most common process in many communities is use of the LiveScan system. This inkless fingerprinting process is typically conducted by appointment at designated locations such as police departments or fire stations. There are generally three separate fees for the fingerprinting: a fee for state-level background check, a fee for the federal-level background check, and a fee to conduct the fingerprinting. Fees for conducting the fingerprinting vary by vendor and typically range from $15-$30. In many areas, mentoring organizations can apply to have the state-level fingerprint check fees waived, and federal-level checks are currently $18. For more information on fingerprinting, contact your local police or sheriff's department. The Megan's Law Database can be accessed online or through various local law enforcement agencies. In California and other areas, agencies may also choose to receive updates in case additional information is added to an applicant's record. For more information on the Sexual Offence Registry for each state, visit the Klaas Kids Foundation at http://www.klaaskids.org.

Process:

During the orientation, attendees should be informed of the background check requirement, as well as any costs which will be incurred by the applicant. In many communities, fingerprinting must be conducted by a representative of the court at an off-site location, while some states allow fingerprinting to be conducted by trained, approved staff. Each state also provides legal parameters regarding the use and documentation of these records. Agencies should have established protocols for referring applicants to local fingerprinting locations, obtaining results, and keeping records. Once agencies verify that applicants do not appear in the Megan's Law Database, staff should follow established procedures for documenting this background check step.

Principles and Protocol for Staff:

Agencies should determine their minimum standards for rejection related to background checks, then ensure that all staff understand these non-negotiable minimums. Each program's legal counsel should be consulted in establishing these minimums, as well as procedures for processing fingerprint results and issues of confidentiality within the organization. Additionally, agencies must comply with current law related to fingerprint documentation, depending on the protocols of the state in which they provide services. Agencies should also implement policies related to dealing with an applicant's disclosure of juvenile record information or violations which do not appear on their fingerprint record. Another consideration is whether or not to permit alternative background checks submissions. For example, applicants may offer to provide background check information from a previous volunteer experience. Another possibility is the use of "background check services," companies which may conduct fingerprinting, Sexual Offender Registry checks, and preliminary screening before referring applicants to youth-serving organization. Because both of these options depend on the effective practices of an organization or company outside of the mentoring program, staff are strongly advised to discuss such alternatives with their legal counsel before utilizing such services. Additional resources and information related to fingerprinting and Sexual Offender Registries are provided in Chapters 8 and 9 of this volume.

In today's technology centered world, there exists another resource for informational checks: use of social media and internet searches. By entering a candidate's name into a search engine, or logging on to a Facebook page, for example, you can see what activities and connections he or she has. Other sites such as YouTube, blogs, and public forums can be accessed. These searches may not only reveal inappropriate activities, but also confirm that the information that they have provided to you throughout the screening process is consistent with what appears on the Internet.

Reflections:

The following descriptions may help your staff members deepen their understanding of issues as they relate to your program's unique needs. They are offered as a starting point for reflection and discussion of situations your agency may encounter. These scenarios and the recommendations of your legal counsel can help you prepare for similar incidents within your program.

- **Background Check Situation 1**

  During the course of the application process, a candidate disclosed that he had served time for sexual assault and possession of narcotics. Neither his state- nor federal-level fingerprint checks came back with any related charges. The candidate was not accepted based on the program's non-negotiable minimum standards for rejection.

- **Background Check Situation 2**

  A candidate had completed all of the application steps except for his fingerprinting. When reminded that this was a required portion of the program's application process, he explained that he was too busy to make a LiveScan appointment. The applicant offered to bring in the results of a previous fingerprint check or to get a copy from the agency with which he had previously volunteered. When the staff explained that these were not acceptable options, the applicant stated that he no longer wished to apply to become a mentor.

Tool: Written Application

The written application is a formal submission of information for use in screening a volunteer applicant.

Components:

The various components of the written application provide staff with a basic profile of a volunteer applicant. This document begins the process of gathering basic information about an applicant, including details about their home, their family, their academic and work history, their legal history and military involvement, and their references. The application is also a starting point for learning about an applicant's values and motivations. It is important that all questions are answered and that the application and release forms are signed. This document is needed to conduct a thorough interview and complete all subsequent screening steps. Chapter 6 will describe the ways in which this information is used, but for the purposes of screening for child predators, several components are particularly important:

- Completion – Has the applicant fully completed the written application, with no omitted answers? Information may be missing for a reason, presenting gaps in an applicant's profile.
- Timing – Was the written application submitted on time? The timing of the application submission can be telling: late applications may reflect problems with an applicant's ability to follow directions, meet deadlines, or follow through on commitments – or this delay may indicate that an applicant is hiding information.
- Content – What is included in the written application? The application content touches upon crucial issues which will be further explored during the interview, and this information begins the process of determining an applicant's motivations for applying to the program.

Process:

The written application form is often provided to applicants during their orientation to the program. Ideally, this form should be completed and returned to the agency before the applicant is interviewed. If the form is submitted during the interview, the staff member should quickly scan the form and assess critical information, including any convictions, counseling or drug history, the applicant's housing/moving history, and past experiences with children. Staff should note any questions which have been left blank or incomplete. If the form is not available at the time of the interview, staff may need to let the applicant know that the interview cannot be conducted or that a secondary interview may be required, depending on the agency's policies.

Principles and Protocol for Staff:

The information omitted from a written application is often as illustrative as the answers provided. Staff should become extremely familiar with the written form, enabling them to quickly ascertain which details warrant further exploration during the interview and character reference checks. By familiarizing themselves with the content of the application, a staff member can more easily listen for interview and reference content which may help to identify a child predator.

Reflections:

The following descriptions may help your staff members deepen their understanding of issues as they relate to your program's unique needs. They are offered as a starting point for reflection and discussion of situations your agency may encounter. These scenarios and the recommendations of your legal counsel can help you prepare for similar incidents within your program.

- **Written Application Situation 1**

  Despite being reminded several times, an applicant did not have her written application completed prior to her in-home interview. The staff member conducting the interview stated that he would need to conduct a secondary interview once the application was submitted, according to the agency policy. At the end of the in-home interview, the applicant and the staff member selected a time when she would come to the office for a brief follow-up session, provided her application had been received.

- **Written Application Situation 2**

  An applicant provided his written application at the time of his in-home interview, and the staff member quickly scanned the form. Several sections of the application were incomplete, including the applicant's last three places of residence and his work history. The staff member changed the order of the interview questions, asking how the applicant liked the neighborhood and whether he had lived in the area for very long. The applicant stated that he had only recently moved to the city and that his work had taken him to several other locations over the past decade. The staff was then able to shift the conversation to the topic of his current employment situation and discovered that he was not currently working because of pending allegations of felony theft from his previous workplace.

Sample
Mentor Application

1.   BACKGROUND INFORMATION

    Name: _____   Gender: _____

    Address: _____

    City: _____   Zip: _____

    Home Phone: (_____) _____   Business Phone:(_____) _____

    Fax/Cell Phone: (_____) _____   Email address: _____

    Age (Optional):_____   Date of Birth (Optional): _____

    Ethnic Background (Optional):_____

    Marital Status_____   Spouse's Name: _____

    Children: _____   Age:_____

    _____   Age:_____

    _____   Age:_____

    _____   Age:_____

    Previous Last Names Used: _____

2.   RESIDENCES

    Please list residences in the last 5 years:

    Address/City/State   Dates

    _____   _____ to _____

    _____   _____ to _____

    _____   _____ to _____

    _____   _____ to _____

    _____   _____ to _____

3.   EDUCATION

    High School: _____   City/State: _____

    Dates Attended: _____ to _____   Graduated? _____

    Post-High School:

    School_____   Major_____   Dates Attended ___ Degree __

    School_____   Major_____   Dates Attended ___ Degree __

    School_____   Major_____   Dates Attended ___ Degree __

4.   MILITARY SERVICE

    Branch   Dates   Type of Discharge

    _____

    _____

    _____

5. JOB HISTORY

    Present Occupation: _____ Dates: _____ to _____

    Work Days and Hours: _____

    Employer: _____

    Address: _____

    Phone: (   ) _____ Ext._____

    Name of Supervisor: _____

    May we call you at work? _____

    If not, why? _____

    This agency may be contacting your employer as a reference.

    Is there any reason that you would not want us to contact your employer?

    If yes, please explain. _____

    _____

    _____

    Last 2 jobs:

    *   Position:_____ Dates: _____ to _____

        Employer: _____

        Address: _____

        Phone: (_____) _____ Ext._____

        Supervisor: _____

        May we contact this employer as a reference? _____

        If not, why? _____

    *   Position:_____ Dates: _____ to _____

        Employer: _____

        Address: _____

        Phone: (_____) _____ Ext._____

        Supervisor: _____

        May we contact this employer as a reference? _____

        If not, why? _____

6. ANTICIPATED FUTURE CHANGES

    Do you know of or have any reasonable expectation of any future change in

    your family status, vocation, or residence? _____

    If yes, please explain. _____

    _____

7. PREVIOUS APPLICATION

    Have you ever previously applied to be a volunteer with this agency? _____

    If yes, please explain. _____

    It is the policy of this agency to not accept applications from candidates

    who have previously applied to and not been accepted by this agency.

8. MEDICAL HISTORY

Major Illness/Medical Problems	Treatment	Dates

Do you take any special medication? _____

If yes, please explain. _____

_____

Have you ever sought counseling or psychological treatment of any type?

_____

If yes, please explain. _____

_____

Have you ever had problems with the use of alcohol or drugs? _____

If yes, please explain. _____

_____

9. TRANSPORTATION

Are you a licensed driver? _____

If yes, do you have your own transportation? _____

Do you carry liability insurance? _____

This agency will need a copy of your insurance certificate for our files.

- Driving Record (Must be completed, in addition to driving record submission)

Infraction	Date

This agency will need a copy of your driving record.

10. REFERENCES

List 4 references, including 1 relative, 1 coworker, and 2 friends you have known for at least 2 years.

1. Name:_____ Relationship: _____

   City, State: _____

   Primary Phone: (_____) _____ ☐ Cell ☐ Business ☐ Home

   Secondary Phone: (_____) _____ ☐ Cell ☐ Business ☐ Home

2. Name:_____　　Relationship: _____
   City, State: _____
   Primary Phone: (_____) _____　☐ Cell ☐ Business ☐ Home
   Secondary Phone: (_____) _____　☐ Cell ☐ Business ☐ Home
3. Name:_____　　Relationship: _____
   City, State: _____
   Primary Phone: (_____) _____　☐ Cell ☐ Business ☐ Home
   Secondary Phone: (_____) _____　☐ Cell ☐ Business ☐ Home
4. Name:_____　　Relationship: _____
   City, State: _____
   Primary Phone: (_____) _____　☐ Cell ☐ Business ☐ Home
   Secondary Phone: (_____) _____　☐ Cell ☐ Business ☐ Home

11. LEGAL HISTORY
    Have you ever been arrested? _____
    If yes, please explain._____

Offense	Date	Action

    Have you ever been investigated/and or charged with child abuse
    or neglect? _____
    If yes, please explain._____
    Have you ever been investigated for and/or charged with crimes against
    children? _____
    If yes, please explain._____

    Have you ever been investigated for and/or charged with assault? _____
    If yes, please explain._____

    Have you ever been investigated for and/or charged with any other
    offenses? _____
    If yes, please explain. _____

12. PERSONAL DATA

What are some values and beliefs that are of special importance to you?

_____
_____
_____

How do you feel these relate to working with young people?

_____
_____
_____

Please list hobbies and activities that you enjoy.

_____
_____
_____

Do you have any special training or skills?

_____
_____
_____

Please list language skills.

_____
_____
_____

Please list any professional memberships, community organization affiliations, etc.

_____
_____
_____

Have you had any experience working with children (volunteer, paid, etc.)?

_____
_____
_____

If yes, please describe.

_____
_____
_____

Additional Comments:

_____
_____
_____

PLEASE READ BEFORE SIGNING:

THE AGENCY does not discriminate against individuals on the basis of race, color, national or ethnic origin, sex, age, religion, disability, veteran status, sexual orientation, gender identity, or economic status.

I hereby apply for membership as a volunteer in **THE AGENCY**. I understand **THE AGENCY** will interview me about my background, motivation, expectations, and other personal qualities that might have a bearing on whether I would be an appropriate volunteer. I agree to supply **THE AGENCY** with a copy of my driving record from the DMV and with proof of automobile insurance. I further agree to submit my information to **THE AGENCY** so that they can conduct a background check, which may include state- and federal-level fingerprint-based searches, the Sexual Offender Registry, and other pertinent Internet searches. I understand that **THE AGENCY** will review references and investigate any and all facts concerning my qualifications for becoming a volunteer. I certify that all of the information provided by me in this application is complete, true, and accurate. I acknowledge that intentional omission or falsification of information will be cause for non-acceptance or immediate dismissal at any time during the period of my placement.

I understand that the agency has to take the best interests of the children into consideration first. Further, I understand that (1) I am not obligated, if called upon, to perform the volunteer services applied for, and (2) THE AGENCY is not obligated to assign or to actively seek to assign me to a volunteer position.

I understand that the statements I make to the staff of the agency will be held confidential within the agency, unless disclosure is required by law. Specifically, I understand that incidents of child abuse or molest, past or present, or threat of harm to oneself or others are issues that must be reported to proper authorities.

I understand that certain information about me will be discussed with the parent/guardian of the child with whom I am matched. If there are things about me that I do not want repeated, it is my responsibility to discuss this with **THE AGENCY** staff.

I agree to keep information discussed with me regarding a potential match confidential. I will not discuss this information with any person other than the assigned professional staff of **THE AGENCY**.

I understand that my application will not be considered unless it is complete and signed and until the required supplemental information is submitted and completed.

I agree to notify **THE AGENCY** immediately of any changes in the information provided in the application process, including, but not limited to, legal status, driving record, employment, address, telephone numbers, name, or marital status. I also agree to maintain automobile insurance during my tenure with **THE AGENC**Y.

This application and any additional information gathered will remain the property of THE AGENCY.

☐ **Yes, I authorize THE AGENCY to use and release any general information and/or photographs acquired by the agency in the context of my association with them for publicity or promotional purposes.**

☐ **No, I do not authorize THE AGENCY to use and release any general information and/or photographs acquired by the agency in the context of my association with them for publicity or promotional purposes.**

Signature: _____ Date: _____
Printed Name of Applicant:_____

MEDICAL RELEASE FORM

I, _____ hereby authorize THE AGENCY to provide access to appropriate emergency medical attention for me. I am allergic to _____ _____ (medications). I have the following medical conditions: (list):
_____

Emergency Contact Information
   Name: _____
   Relationship: _____
   Phone Daytime: (_____) _____ Evening: (_____) _____
   Name: _____
   Relationship: _____
   Phone Daytime: (_____) _____ Evening: (_____) _____
Signature: _____ Date: _____
Print Name: _____
Home Address: _____
Phone Numbers: _____
Additional Information: _____
_____
_____
_____

Copyright © Friends for Youth 2014

Tool: Interview

The interview is the heart of the screening process. It is a one-to-one or one-to-several staff process during which staff members gather information on the life, lifestyle, history, and personality of an applicant.

Components:

The various components of the interview delve into each stage and aspect of an applicant's life, including his or her history, schooling, work and private life, interests, and personality. The interview should cover the candidate's life from childhood to the present. Chapter 6 will describe the ways in which this information is used, but for the purposes of screening for child predators, several interview components are particularly important:

- Motivation – Why does this individual want to volunteer in the program?
- History of Abuse – Was the applicant abused as a child? Is there a history of abuse within the family? Most importantly, what type of support did he or she receive to help them heal from their experience?
- Support Network – Who are the applicant's peers? With whom does he or she spend time?
- Experience With Children – Is there a pattern of involvement in activities involving children?
- Preferences – Is the applicant specific about the type of child he or she would like to mentor? Do they place significant emphasis on the physical or emotional characteristics of the mentee?

Process:

The interview is crucial in exploring the motivations and history of a volunteer applicant, and this process should not be rushed. Ideally, the interview takes place within the mentor's home; if it takes place elsewhere, a separate home visit should be scheduled. When arriving at the applicant's home, it is useful to have a tour of the home at the beginning of the interview. This provides staff with details which may be useful during the interview, such as the types of videos, photos, or art within the home. For community-based mentoring programs, it also provides topics to later discuss regarding child safety issues (such as safety around a swimming pool or a high-rise balcony). At the start of the interview, the staff member should remind the applicant that the process is part of both the agency's screening and matching processes. With a blank copy of the interview form, the staff member should carefully follow the interview topics and exactly document the applicant's wording. If the applicant begins to significantly change the direction of the conversation, the interviewer should redirect the conversation so that no interview topics are overlooked or skipped. At the same time, the staff member should also be attentive to candidates who may be answering the question properly but in a way that may not be typical. Staff should also be trained on and practice exceptional listening skills, as candidates may naturally morph conversations into other facets of their lives that are relevant and important to be covered in the interview. As the interview is ending, the staff member should ask whether there are any important topics that have not been discussed, giving the interviewee an opportunity to disclose other information or ask questions about the mentor screening process. Immediately following the interview, the staff member should document their personal reactions to the candidate and the interview, as well as any behaviors or non-verbal communication exhibited by the candidate. The information gathered through the interview should be shared with other direct service staff members who may play a role in the decision of whether a candidate will be accepted as a mentor.

Principles and Protocol for Staff:

It is vital that staff members thoroughly document applicant responses, using as close to the exact wording as possible. Remember, child predators become very skilled at charming and manipulating others. Thorough and complete documentation is critical so that staff members can later review the interview form, read the responses, and identify whether the candidate actually answered the questions that were asked. Staff should also note whether candidates provide too much information, not enough information, or vague details. The interview form should also reflect if a candidate becomes emotional and whether that reaction seemed appropriate (e.g., becoming tearful when sharing details of the loss of a parent) or inappropriate (e.g., becoming visibly disassociated or agitated while stating that she had a wonderful childhood). After the interview, reviewing the interview form allows staff to note their feelings during the conversation and whether the candidate attempted to redirect or misdirect the conversation. Allowing sufficient time to complete this review can help staff members gain perspective on the interview, with an opportunity to recognize issues which may need further exploration. The interview can provide staff with insights into an applicant's motivations, life, and skills, as well as reflecting how well he or she interacts with other adults. Because this process should not be rushed, it is sometimes difficult to schedule into a specific time period, such as during a lunch break or before the applicant goes to work. If the interview cannot be completed to the staff's satisfaction, another time should be scheduled to resume the conversation, rather than completing it over the phone or in written form. During the course of the interview, staff may encounter a response or a situation which immediately disqualifies the candidate or makes the staff member uncomfortable with ever matching the candidate with a child. Staff should be prepared with a modified interview form or series of questions so that the interview can be quickly terminated. It is important to note that, unlike a job application process, there are no questions or topics which cannot legally be broached with volunteer applicants. This can be clarified further by your legal counsel.

Reflections:

The following descriptions may help your staff members deepen their understanding of issues as they relate to your program's unique needs. They are offered as a starting point for reflection and discussion of situations your agency may encounter. These scenarios and the recommendations of your legal counsel can help you prepare for similar incidents within your program.

- **Interview Situation 1**

  During the course of an interview, the staff member asked a female applicant how she felt about her childhood. The woman stated that she did not want to talk about her childhood. When encouraged to share whether it had been a difficult time in her life, she demanded to know why she had to answer the question and refused to continue discussing the subject. The staff member explained that questions were asked to help uncover what types of mentee needs she might be able to best support. The candidate then provided a brief, vague response.

- **Interview Situation 2**

  Midway through an interview, a candidate mentioned how glad he was to be working with children again since he had not been able to volunteer at Agency A or Z. He disclosed that he had a series of recent drunk driving convictions and had been arrested for possession of a controlled substance. According to agency policy, the staff member could not disclose to the candidate that these issues would disqualify him from becoming a mentor. Rather than continue with the entire interview, the staff member followed a modified version. This modified version included several bolded topics on the original form, highlighting only the most general pieces of information.

Sample
Applicant Interview

Applicant Name: _____   Interview Date: _____
Referral Source: _____   Interviewed By: _____

OPENING REMARKS
Explain the purpose of the interview: part of the screening process as well as a major portion of the matching process. Describe how the interview will examine different aspects of the applicant's life in an effort to see how he/she would work in the program and what types of experiences might help support a mentee. Obtain feedback on the orientation session and answer any questions.

COMMITMENT REQUIREMENTS
Review minimum time requirements for being a mentor.
1. Are you comfortable with the program's three hour a week commitment? Are you able to make a commitment to your mentee for one year from the time you meet?

MOTIVATION
2. Why are you interested in being a mentor? Why are you interested in working with children?

VOLUNTEER EXPERIENCE
3. What kinds of past volunteer experiences have you had? What did you like/dislike about them?
4. Are you currently looking into any other volunteer programs? Are you already a volunteer with any other programs?

EXPERIENCE WITH YOUTH
5. Tell me about any children in your life (sons/daughters, nieces/nephews, friends, grandchildren).
6. Have you had experience working with children? What ages? What did you do? How would you describe your experiences?
7. How connected do you feel to youth culture today?

FAMILY HISTORY

8. Where were you born and raised?

9. How would you describe your personality as a child and as a teen? What kinds of activities did you enjoy?

10. Who was in your family? What are the ages of your siblings? What was your relationship like with them as a child? And today?

11. What was your relationship like with each of your parents as a child? And today?

12. Please describe your father's personality and your mother's personality.

13. Did both of your parents work while you were growing up? What did they do for a living?

14. Were there extended family members who were a part of your childhood?

15. How was affection displayed in your family? How was communication exhibited? How were you disciplined?

16. Were there any major changes or stresses (economic, illnesses, etc.) as you were growing up? Overall, how do you feel about your childhood?

17. How might you use your experience to connect with your mentee?

EDUCATIONAL HISTORY

18. Describe your overall experience of school (relationships with your peers and teachers, school performance, extracurricular activities). What was the highest level of education you obtained?

19. What, if any, problems did you have in school?

20. What motivated you? Do you have any future educational plans that involve moving out of the area?

21. What are your expectations around your mentee's achievement and motivation levels?

JOB HISTORY

22. Where do you work? What is your current position? How long have you been there?

23. What are your relationships like with your supervisor and coworkers?

24. What has been satisfying/frustrating about your current job? What are your career goals?

25. What was your first job ever? How old were you? What kind of experience was it?

26. Briefly highlight your jobs from your first job through today. Why did you change/leave jobs?

SOCIAL RELATIONSHIP HISTORY

27. What is your marital status?

28. If in a relationship, could you briefly describe this relationship (interaction, future plans, length of relationship)? What is the age and occupation of your spouse/significant other? How does your spouse/significant other feel about your involvement with this program? Will your spouse/significant other be involved?

    Explain need for screening prior to leaving the child in spouse's care, as well as the fact that this is a topic further covered during the volunteer training.

29. Please briefly describe any previous significant relationships.

30. If divorced or separated, for how long? How long were you married? In general, what precipitated the divorce/separation? How have you adjusted to the divorce/separation? Currently, how is your relationship with your ex-spouse?

31. Do you have any children? What are their ages and gender? What is your relationship like with them? How do they feel about your involvement with this program?

32. What does friendship mean to you?

33. Describe your social circle. Who are your close friends (age, gender, length of friendship)?

34. What do you with your friends? Do you participate in any clubs or activities?

35. What experience do you have with other cultures? Do you speak any other languages?

36. How do you handle stress or crisis? Would you do anything different for stress or crisis in your personal life versus career?

37. How would you approach being matched with a mentee whose life experience is very different from your own (i.e., knows/interacts only with own culture, divorced parents, grandparents as guardians, general dysfunction)?

RELIGIOUS/SPIRITUAL HISTORY

38. Did you have a religious upbringing? Do you practice any religion today? Which one? How active are you?

MILITARY HISTORY

39. Do you have any military experience? Please describe your experience (length, type of service, nature of discharge, etc.)?

LIVING SITUATION

40. How long have you been living here? Where else have you lived? Do you have any plans to move?

41. Who else lives with you? What are their genders, ages, and occupations? Are they supportive of your involvement with this program? Will they be involved?
    If they plan to be an active part of the mentoring relationship, describe the necessary process.

42. Do you have any pets? What are their names?

43. Do have guns or other weapons in your home? How many and what kinds of weapons are in the home? Where are they kept?

44. Do you have any adult-only materials such as alcohol, cigarettes, drugs, magazines, or movies in your home? Where are they kept?
    If so, explain the need to be out of the mentee's access.

45. Are there any potential hazards (e.g., pools, Jacuzzis, balconies, special equipment) in your home or neighborhood? How will you protect your mentee?

46. Please describe your neighborhood. Do you feel safe here?

47. Some of our mentees live in neighborhoods that have high gang activity, drug commerce, or are generally lower-income. Do you have any concerns about driving into a place like this?

LEGAL HISTORY

48. Do you have any legal history such as accusations, arrests, investigations, charges, police involvement, infractions, altercations, etc.? Do you have any child abuse legal history?

49. Do you have any traffic violations? Do you have any DUIs/DWIs?

50. Have you ever been the victim of a crime, abusive behavior, or any other such action? If yes, how did/do you cope with this experience?

51. How would you feel if you were matched with a mentee who had a legal history or had been victimized?

DRUG/ALCOHOL HISTORY

52. Have you or do you have any history of drug or alcohol use or abuse? What are your views and practices in regards to tobacco, drug, and alcohol use?

53. How would you feel if you were matched with a mentee who had experimented with substances?

MEDICAL HISTORY

54. Have you ever been hospitalized for a serious illness? Do you have any health conditions? Are you taking any prescription or non-prescription medication?

HOBBIES/INTERESTS

55. Please describe your hobbies and interests.

56. Have you thought about what you might want to do with your mentee?

57. Do you have any scheduling conflicts that would affect when you meet with your mentee?

PREFERENCES

58. Geographic limits

59. Gender

60. Age

61. Ethnicity/Religion

62. Is there any situation in which your mentee might be in that would make you uncomfortable (e.g., gang involvement, abusive environment, or suicide attempts)?

CLOSURE

63. What are you hoping to get out of this experience? What do you hope your mentee gets out of this experience?

64. What qualifies you to become a mentor in this program?

65. Is there anything else that would be helpful for me to know?
66. Do you have any concerns or questions?

REVIEW APPLICATION PROCESS
- Written Application
- Interview
- Fingerprints (submitted and cleared)
- Driving record
- Proof of auto insurance
- References (included in written application)
- Training
  Remind applicant that acceptance is based on the Selection Committee's review of the entire application packet and that all reasons for decisions are confidential. All applicants may be rejected at anytime in the application process.

Interviewer Comments _____

Tool: References

Character references are utilized to gain additional insight into the candidate's personality and motivations, as well as to verify the accuracy of information presented by the applicant.

Components:

The various components of the reference check are used to further explore the applicant's history, schooling, work and private life, interests, and personality. Chapter 6 will describe the ways in which this information is used, but for the purposes of screening for child predators, several reference check components are particularly important:

- Reference Selection – Are the selected references appropriate?
- History – How long have the references known the applicant? How well do they know him or her? Do the references represent an appropriate spectrum of the candidate's life?
- Believability – How honest and believable are the references? Are they providing accurate information or the information they think the program wants to hear?
- Motivation and Match – What do the references think are the applicant's motivations for becoming a mentor? Who do the references think would be an ideal match for the applicant?
- Consistency – Is the information provided by the references consistent with the applicant's information and the impressions of the staff?
- Hinting – Are the references "hinting" or indirectly providing additional information, based on what they say, what they do not say, or how they convey information?

Process:

Reference checks are an opportunity to view applicants through the perspectives of different people. Agencies should require an adequate number of references to help build a complete picture of an applicant: this is typically four references, including family, friends, and coworkers. It is significantly more effective to conduct oral (telephone) references than to use written references. This use of verbal communication allows staff to gauge tone and perspective, as well as to clarify questions or follow up on comments. When conducting reference checks, staff should clearly introduce themselves and the agency to which the candidate is applying. It is also useful to briefly describe the actual role the applicant could be playing within the agency. As a courtesy, staff should provide references with a time frame (e.g., 5 to 10 minutes) for the reference check conversation. It is also important to let references know that their responses will be kept confidential and that the information is used as part of the program's screening and matching processes. The reference check conversation should use open-ended questions, and staff should carefully document the responses. It is also recommended that staff provide their contact number, in case a reference thinks of any additional information.

Principles and Protocol for Staff:

Because it can be time-consuming to track down references, it is logical that this step takes place near the end of the application process and only for the most promising applicants. Reference checks are challenging: staff must quickly introduce the program, describe the reference check process, set the reference at ease, and gather useful information. It is vital that staff become comfortable with the reference check process and be flexible in pursuing details which the reference may feel are important to disclose. Staff should learn to listen carefully for both direct and indirect information. Indirect information may be conveyed when the reference is vague, hesitates before answering, or is non-committal. During the conversation, a reference's tone of voice or level of nervousness should also be documented. In conducting references, staff should not be afraid to probe for more complete answers. It is useful for new staff to practice conducting mock reference checks before contacting actual references. Ideally, staff members will exchange information related to the orientation, application, and interview before the reference checks are conducted. This allows for an opportunity to follow up on questions or issues which were generated during the earlier stages of the candidate's application process. Because of the complexity and confidentiality of conducting character reference checks, it is not generally appropriate for volunteers to assist with this task.

Reflections:

The following descriptions may help your staff members deepen their understanding of issues as they relate to your program's unique needs. They are offered as a starting point for reflection and discussion of situations your agency may encounter. These scenarios and the recommendations of your legal counsel can help you prepare for similar incidents within your program.

- **Reference Check Situation 1**

  During the interview, a candidate stated that he had become estranged from his brother after the death of their father. When asked for references, the candidate provided four young women who had each known him for less than six months. The program coordinator asked for someone who had known him for a longer period of time and reminded the applicant that one family member was also needed. The candidate provided a phone number for his "brother" who was easily contacted and offered a glowing recommendation. Much of his information, however, did not match that provided by the applicant, including comments related to their relationship and current level of communication.

- **Reference Check Situation 2**

  An applicant provided her adult daughter as a reference. When contacted, the staff member briefly explained that their conversation would be confidential and that references played an important role in ensuring a safe mentoring experience for at-risk youth mentees. The daughter said that she was concerned about her mother's current ability to make appropriate decisions with a young person. She also stated that her mother was a terrible, distracted driver who had "no business being on the road." For the emotional and physical safety of a child, she would not recommend ever approving her mother as a mentor.

Sample
Volunteer Mentor Reference Check

1. Purpose of call: Explain that applicant is interested in volunteering for **THE AGENCY** as a mentor, has listed him/her as a reference, and you need to ask him/her a few questions as part of our standard screening process. Make sure that he/she has about 5-10 minutes to talk.

2. Explain the confidentiality waiver: all information given is shared only with Program Staff and Selection Committee, and will not be shared with the applicant.

3. Ask reference if he/she is familiar with **THE AGENCY**. If not, explain program.

4.　Begin questions:

How long have you known the applicant? How well do you know the applicant?

How often do you communicate with each other?

Have you seen the applicant working or interacting with youth? What was that like?

How do you think the applicant would work in our program? Why is that?

Why do you think the applicant wants to be involved with THE AGENCY?

How is the applicant in following through with commitments? Do you think the applicant will have any problem making a one-year commitment to a youth?

How would the applicant work with different ethnic groups?

Would the applicant be open to suggestions about relating to a young person or if any problems come up?

Do you have any hesitations in recommending him/her as an applicant?

Do you have any suggestions on matching the applicant, in terms of interests or preferences?

Is there anything else you can think of that would be helpful for me to know?

5.　Thank the reference for his/her time and ask if he/she is interested in volunteering or getting more info about **THE AGENCY**.

6.　Leave your name and contact information in case the reference thinks of anything else to share.

Copyright © Friends for Youth 2014

Tool: Driving Record and Proof of Insurance

The Driving Record is an official record of an applicant's file from the Department of Motor Vehicles. Proof of Insurance is physical confirmation that the applicant has current coverage on his or her automobile.

Components:

As stated earlier, SAFE does not focus on all the critical elements required for screening and monitoring volunteers. Instead, this manual specifically focuses on identifying potential child predators who may be applying to a youth-serving organization. In this sense, the Driving Record and Proof of Insurance offer an opportunity to discuss specific topics with a volunteer applicant, as well as to verify the validity of application material. Chapter 6 will describe the ways in which this information is used, but for the purposes of screening for child predators, several Driving Record and Proof of Insurance components are particularly important:

- Consistency – Does all of the information contained on the Driving Record and Proof of Insurance match with other information presented by the applicant?
- History – How long has the applicant lived in the state from which the Driving Record was obtained? If the applicant's in-state residency has been brief, is there another state from which additional information should be requested?
- Content – Is there content on the Driving Record or related to the Proof of Insurance which might call into questions the applicant's honesty or actions? For example, are there violations which involve drugs or alcohol, or are there coverage increases related to inappropriate use of the automobile?

Process:

An applicant's Driving Record and Proof of Insurance offer opportunities to verify information presented by a potential volunteer. Depending on an agency's legal counsel, programs may require that these documents be submitted either by the applicant or by official means (i.e., directly from the Department of Motor Vehicles and the insurance company). Staff should obtain a "code list" from both the Department of Motor Vehicles and the insurance company so that all items on the submitted documents may be identified and verified.

Principles and Protocol for Staff:

Information included on these documents – particularly if not included elsewhere in material presented by an applicant – provides insight into both the character and the activities of the potential volunteer. Staff should become extremely familiar with codes found on these documents, enabling them to quickly ascertain which details will warrant further exploration during the interview and reference checks. Agencies should also have a very clear policy regarding the use of information contained in these documents, both for the sake of selecting appropriate mentors (not covered by SAFE) and for issues related to potential child predators. It is useful for agencies to remember that infractions may be removed/expunged from Driving Records, perhaps after a specified length of time or as a result of attending driving school.

Reflections:

The following descriptions may help your staff members deepen their understanding of issues as they relate to your program's unique needs. They are offered as a starting point for reflection and discussion of situations your agency may encounter. These scenarios and the recommendations of your legal counsel can help you prepare for similar incidents within your program.

- **Driving Record/Insurance Situation 1**
  An applicant who had been slow to submit her Driving Record finally brought the document to the agency. The record contained seven infractions. The applicant had not listed these infractions under the written application driving record question, and she had not mentioned them during her interview. The program coordinator reviewing her Driving Record documented his concerns regarding her honesty.

- **Driving Record/Insurance Situation 2**
  Although he stated that he has lived in the area for several years, an applicant's driving record only contained material from the past six months. Upon being questioned, the applicant explained that he never updated his old driving record, choosing instead to carry an out-of-state license while he resided locally. When the program coordinator explained that additional driving information would be required for the safety of the youth participants, the applicant became argumentative and derided the "stupid policy."

Tool: Volunteer Training

Volunteer training is a designated group setting in which agencies provide data, training, and feedback related to situations which may be encountered by candidates during their volunteer experience.

Components:

One of the final screening steps is typically attendance at a volunteer training session. This is an opportunity to observe how a candidate responds to materials related to their volunteer role, how they interact with other candidates, and how they present themselves to staff. Again, SAFE does not focus on all the critical elements required to effectively train volunteer mentors. Instead, this volume specifically focuses on issues related to identifying child predators who may be applying to youth-serving organizations. In this sense, the volunteer training serves as a laboratory to observe how a candidate responds to topics and interacts with adults. Chapter 6 will describe the ways in which this information is used, but for the purposes of screening for child predators, several volunteer training components are particularly important:

- Questions – What types of questions does the applicant ask? Are they appropriate for the setting and the situation?
- Comfort – How comfortably does the applicant interact with his or her peers?
- Communication– Is the candidate able to communicate with others, including the staff members present at the session?
- Responses – How does the candidate respond to the scenarios presented? Are his or her responses inappropriate, atypical, or unusual? In particular, how does the applicant respond during the review of policies and procedures? Does he or she ask any inappropriate, atypical, or unusual questions?
- Reaction – What type of personal reactions do staff have to the applicant? What type of observed personal reactions do other participants have to a particular applicant?

Process:

The volunteer training is often an agency's last opportunity to observe how a candidate behaves with peers and program staff. Although not explored in this volume, volunteer training sessions generally cover several topics which could offer insight into the motivations of the candidate, particularly successful mentoring practices, the role of a mentor, youth development issues, the needs of specific youth populations, mentor expectations, setting boundaries, communication skills, how culture can impact a mentoring relationship, program requirements, and mentor responsibilities. By carefully designing activities and facilitating discussions, staff can engage applicants and observe their behaviors. Volunteer trainings which depend primarily on lecture may be useful for conveying information to applicants, but they provide little feedback to staff who are screening for potential child predators. At the conclusion of the training, staff should document and share their reactions to the group and to each individual candidate.

Principles and Protocol for Staff:

At this point, it may be tempting for staff to begin thinking of the candidates as "waiting volunteers." It is important to realize that the volunteer training session is still part of the pre-match screening process, and it provides an opportunity to observe and explore the motivations and interactions of each applicant. Staff should be comfortable enough with the training material to use flexibility in conducting activities. For example, if an agency's training includes scenarios for candidates to discuss in pairs and then present to the group, the staff member should be familiar with all available scenarios, possibly distributing specific scenarios (with discretion) to specific volunteer candidates. Staff should learn to listen and watch carefully for both direct and indirect information. This includes body language, changes in tone or voice, and recognizing tension or agitation. Ideally, staff members will exchange information and impressions prior to the volunteer training, allowing the trainer to watch for specific behaviors. Staff should also be skilled in conflict avoidance/resolution. This includes an ability to effectively address or deflect the inappropriate comments or behaviors of one candidate so as not to jeopardize the participation of all volunteer training attendees.

Reflections:

The following descriptions may help your staff members deepen their understanding of issues as they relate to your program's unique needs. They are offered as a starting point for reflection and discussion of situations your agency may encounter. These scenarios and the recommendations of your legal counsel can help you prepare for similar incidents within your program.

- **Volunteer Training Situation 1**

   During the volunteer training, a candidate expresses his displeasure at a Mentor Code of Conduct rule against overnight activities. This candidate enjoys camping, and he insists that "the rugged outdoors" helps young people to develop new skills and interests. He had previously raised this issue during the scenarios activity by offering a camping trip as a solution to help diffuse tension in the home of his potential mentee. As the candidate became agitated by the discussion, the program coordinator briefly thanked him for his feedback, promising to pass his comments on to the agency's decision-making body. She then quickly moved on to the next item on the Mentor Code of Conduct.

- **Volunteer Training Situation 2**

  One of the candidates at a volunteer training appeared visibly uncomfortable during the session, particularly when working on activities conducted in pairs. At lunchtime, the other five candidates selected their "lunchboxes" and returned to the table for the half-hour break. The uncomfortable candidate mumbled his apologies, then left the training to run errands. He returned when the training was to resume.

Tool: Final Decision

Once the screening process steps are completed, the final decision serves as an opportunity for staff and other members of a program's selection committee to discuss a candidate's full application and all interactions with that applicant.

Components:

This step is the final pre-match component of the Objective Data phase, serving as the bridge to the Informed Intuition phase of volunteer screening. The final decision process ideally involves all staff and other members of a program's selection committee who have interacted with the candidate; if the candidate has been referred by one of these individuals, an agency may wish to exclude them from the final decision process. This process should review and encompass every contact, communication, and screening step of the candidate, from the initial recruitment contact to the references, interview, and training. A final decision of acceptance into the program should never occur until all screening and application steps are completed, but a rejection/disqualification may take place prior to completing this process. Although the final decision process may also include additional topics related to whether a candidate is appropriate for a specific mentoring program, this volume focuses specifically on those topics related to screening for child predators. Chapter 6 will describe additional ways to utilize application materials to establish a final decision, but several issues are particularly important in screening applicants:

- Reaction and Intuition – What type of personal reactions have staff had to the applicant? Do staff or other members of the program's selection committee have any negative or uneasy intuitive feelings about the candidate?
- Consistency – Does the candidate's application material appear consistent and align well with itself?
- No Accommodations – Has the candidate completed the application process without any special accommodations from staff?
- Fit – Does the candidate and his or her interests, motivations, and overall application material "fit" with the agency's goals and objectives?
- Concerns – Do staff have any concern about putting a child into the care of the candidate?
- Does the candidate make special requests or suggestions such as wanting to meet the child first?

Process:

As a group, the staff and others selection committee members responsible for screening and matching should meet privately to review candidates who have completed their application process. For each candidate, the staff member who has conducted the majority of the candidate's application steps should briefly highlight the application for the group, verifying that each of the steps has been completed. An agency checklist is typically used to document that this verification has occurred. All staff members who have interacted with the candidate should share their experience of the applicant and their overall impressions of the individual. If the group feels that it needs additional information or that the process is incomplete, review of the candidate should be postponed until all application material is completed. Ideally, the program will have established protocols regarding the final decision, and these will have been briefly reviewed during each orientation session. Candidates who receive a positive response to the final decision should be notified of their acceptance into the program, based on the agency's established process. For candidates who have been rejected, the agency should follow the protocols described during the orientation session. This typically includes a formal letter thanking the applicant for their interest, explaining that their services will not be required, and reminding them that the reasons for rejection are confidential and non-negotiable.

Principles and Protocol for Staff:

Staff should always remember who their program's beneficiaries are: it is the responsibility of mentoring programs to ensure the safety and well-being of each mentee. This may sometimes result in the disqualification of adult applicants who initially appeared to be appropriate candidates or who connected well with one or more of the agency's staff members. It is the purpose of the final decision process to ensure that no staff or selection committee members have any hesitation about a candidate. This should not be a "majority rule" or even a "quorum" decision: mentor approvals should always be unanimous. Because of the nature of decline letters, omitting the signature of any one staff person may be received as less of a personal rejection – potentially helping to diffuse any disgruntled contact by these individuals. Should a rejected candidate contact the agency, programs should be prepared with a process to reiterate the agency's policies regarding applicant declines.

Reflections:

The following descriptions may help your staff members deepen their understanding of issues as they relate to your program's unique needs. They are offered as a starting point for reflection and discussion of situations your agency may encounter. These scenarios and the recommendations of your legal counsel can help you prepare for similar incidents within your program.

- **Final Decision Situation 1**

    Throughout the process, one staff member completed most of a candidate's application steps: he conducted the orientation, the interview, and the training. Because the agency had a policy of candidates meeting with more than one staff member, another program coordinator arranged to talk briefly with the candidate when he delivered his driving record to the office. She told the candidate that their "mini meeting" could be useful during the matching process. She also completed the candidate's reference checks. The initial staff person described the candidate as "a great guy and a jokester." The second staff person, however, was extremely uncomfortable with the candidate, finding him to be "creepy and odd." She also felt that the references did not know the candidate well. The agency's decline letter was sent to the candidate, thanking him for his interest but stating that he had not been accepted into the program. The letter was sent from "The Selection Committee," and the candidate did not contact the agency after receiving the letter.

- **Final Decision Situation 2**

    After sending its rejection letter, the agency received an angry telephone call from a candidate. The candidate called the staff person who had completed his interview. According to agency policy, all calls from rejected candidates are to be routed to the Program Director. The Program Director listened to the angry candidate then calmly explained that staff were not able to discuss any issues related to the Selection Committee's final decision. The candidate continued to demand to know why he had been rejected. The Program Director referred the candidate to the Executive Director, who reminded the candidate that, as explained during the orientation, all reasons for rejection are confidential. The candidate then asked to speak with the Board of Directors. The Executive Director told the candidate that he could write a letter which would be relayed to the appropriate Board member. The candidate did submit a letter. The Executive Director met with the Board Chair to briefly update her on the incident. The Board Chair asked the Executive Director to convey her thanks to all staff involved in the application process, commending them for their role in ensuring the safety of the program's youth participants.

Sample
Volunteer Assessment/Final Decision
Conversation Guide (INTERNAL ONLY)

PRESENCE
- ☐ Housing situation
- ☐ Employment/financial outlook
- ☐ Future plans

STABILITY
- ☐ Mental/emotional health
- ☐ Stable sense of self

ATTITUDE
- ☐ Unconditional regard
- ☐ Nurturing presence
- ☐ Persistence, tenacity, not give up
- ☐ Acceptance of potential mentee as is
- ☐ Empathy, listening, understanding
- ☐ Ability to forge alliance
- ☐ Cultural sensitivity/experience

ACTIONS
- ☐ Setting limits, ability to be firm & direct
- ☐ Setting goals
- ☐ Encouraging of potential mentee's interests/self-exploration
- ☐ Ability to remain positive in negative situations
- ☐ Willingness to get involved in helping youth/community
- ☐ Acceptance of adult/role model responsibility
- ☐ Understanding of and cooperation with program guidelines

PREFERENCES
- ☐ Geographic location of potential mentee
- ☐ Gender
- ☐ Age
- ☐ Interests
- ☐ Uncomfortable situations

Copyright © Friends for Youth 2014

Sample
Volunteer Acceptance Guidelines
(INTERNAL)

1. Applicant must have a good driving record. Every applicant must supply a copy of his/her entire DMV driving record to [AGENCY].

2. Applicant must have a valid driver's license and car insurance that meets the minimum requirements for the state of [STATE]. Proof of insurance must be supplied.

3. Applicants with a history of frequent moving must sufficiently explain each transition. Applicant must plan to live in the area for the required time commitment.

4. Applicant must show a stable employment record. Employment references may be contacted.

5. If the applicant has any history of drug, alcohol, emotional or other problems, it must be shown that he/she received treatment, and sufficient time must have passed in order for the recovery to be complete.

6. Applicant must show a balance in extra-curricular activities.

7. Applicant must complete [Live Scan] fingerprinting for both a state and federal criminal history background check. Applicant may not have committed any felonies and may not have any record of assault or violent behavior. If a misdemeanor appears, it will be evaluated on an individual basis. Under no circumstances will any applicant be accepted who has ever been suspected of, investigated for, charged with, or convicted of crimes concerning children such as child molestation, abuse, neglect, etc.

8. Applicant must supply [AGENCY] with all information that is required in the application and interview process. The information must be consistent.

9. Volunteers whose matches do not work out will be re-evaluated before matching them again.

10. Staff – based on their interactions and intuition — must not have any safety concerns or sense of uneasiness about the applicant.

Copyright © Friends for Youth 2014

Tool: Ongoing Monitoring

As thoroughly as an agency may implement its screening processes, it is possible for a child molester to infiltrate a program. He or she will then slowly and subtly begin the grooming process before molesting the mentee. Therefore, the "screening" process continues even after a mentor is matched with a young person. Ongoing monitoring of relationships includes direct communication, observations, and contact with the mentor, the mentee, his or her family, and referring agents or school officials.

Components:

Ongoing monitoring includes all forms of communication (face-to-face contact, telephone conversations, e-mails) which take place after a match has occurred. It includes feedback from the mentor, as well as information from the mentee, the child's family or caregiver, and his or her teacher or referral agent. Staff observations of the pair when they are together also offer crucial information. Chapter 6 will describe the ways in which these interactions are used, but for the purposes of screening for child predators, several concepts are particularly important:

- Comfort – How comfortable does the child and his or her family seem to be with the mentor? Does the mentor seem overly comfortable or inappropriate with the mentee?

- Interactions – Is the mentor appropriate in his or her physical or verbal interactions with the mentee?

- Activities and Time – In what types of activities do the mentor and mentee engage? Do their activities involve interaction with other people (e.g., attending a school carnival or seeing a jazz concert), or do they typically include long periods of time alone (such as hiking, "hanging out," or watching television)? If their time is not spent in the company of other people, does the pair exceed the program's recommended or requested amount of time together, or do activities occur at times not generally appropriate for a young person?

- Secrecy – Have staff or the child's family noticed that the child has an excessive number of "secrets" related to their mentoring relationship? Is there an air of secrecy or an unusual number of private glances between the mentor and mentee? Even in group settings, do the mentor and mentee remain separate from the rest of the group in some way?

- Change – Have the child's family, teachers, or referring agent noticed a negative or unsocial change in the child?

- Cooperation – Does the mentor continue to follow the agency's rules, recommendations, and regulations? If a potential problem is identified, how does the mentor react to staff suggestions? Is the mentor cooperative in returning calls and fulfilling the commitments of a mentor within the program's structure?
- Consistency – Are the activity reports of the mentor consistent with those provided by the mentee, the mentee's family, and the mentee's referring agent or teacher? Are the perceptions and experience of their time spent together similar for both the mentor and the mentee?

Process:

The screening process does not end once a volunteer has been accepted into a program. In fact, this is only the beginning of a new form of screening. Child molesters rarely abuse children immediately. They first develop a close bond with the young person and gain the trust of all those involved. This process takes time. Ongoing monitoring must be incorporated into the program system. Although not detailed in this volume, the basic monitoring activities which should be implemented to address the potential for child predators include

- Weekly or bi-weekly staff contact with both mentors and mentees;
- Three-month or mid-year reviews which take place face-to-face and involve separate interviews with the mentor, the mentee, and the mentee's parent or guardian;
- Watching for behavioral changes of the mentee or the mentor;
- Observing mentor/mentee pairs at group activities, life skills workshops, and social events;
- Ongoing and consistent contact with parents or guardians;
- Year-end match review, with staff guidance on agency closure policies; and
- Alumni tracking process.

Principles and Protocol for Staff:

Even after a match has occurred, staff must remain focused on ensuring a safe, positive relationship for mentees. Careful documentation and regular contact with all parties (mentors, mentees, family members, teachers, and referring agents) helps to ensure that the relationship is progressing appropriately. Staff should clearly document their communications and interactions with the pair, their family, and other parties observing the mentee. It is also important that staff continue to share their interactions with coworkers, particularly if a variety of staff members observe mentor/mentee pairs during group outings or workshops. Agencies should have a clear process in place for intervening with or terminating relationships in a way which is not detrimental to the mentee. In particular, agencies should prepare their staff for situations in which sexual abuse is suspected; for further details on how on how to handle sexual abuse disclosure and sexual abuse reporting, please see Chapter 10.

Reflections:

The following descriptions may help your staff members deepen their understanding of issues as they relate to your program's unique needs. They are offered as a starting point for reflection and discussion of situations your agency may encounter. These scenarios and the recommendations of your legal counsel can help you prepare for similar incidents within your program.

- **Ongoing Monitoring Situation 1**

  An agency's new program coordinator received a call from a mentee's parent. Her son had been matched for about a year, but she had had little contact with staff for several months. The mentor was coordinating a camping trip for her son, and the mother was unsure of the policies regarding overnights or even the status of her son in the program. The program coordinator explained that the family's initial staff contact person had recently left the agency. She promised to the mother call back within the hour with more details. After hanging up the phone, the program coordinator quickly reviewed the file and asked her coworkers for any feedback on the pair, for a review of the agency's policy for overnights, and for information on procedures and rules regarding "alumni" (pairs which complete the program's one-year commitment period).

- **Ongoing Monitoring Situation 2**

  Shortly after being matched with his mentor, a mentee called his program coordinator to ask about upcoming activities. These group activities are optional recreational activities and workshops for mentor/mentee pairs. Together, over the phone, the program coordinator and the mentee reviewed their copies of the monthly newsletter of activities. The mentee asked to sign up for an activity, and the program coordinator said that he and his mentor could attend. A month later, the mentee again called. The program coordinator asked why he did not come to the activity, and the mentee explained that his mentor had made other plans for the two of them. The mentee asked to sign up for another activity, but again the pair did not attend on the day of the outing. The program coordinator arranged to visit the mentee and discovered that the mentor was choosing different outings on the days of the group activities. She contacted the mentor to further explore why the mentor seemed to be avoiding group settings with his mentee.

Sample
Ongoing Monitoring Questions

QUESTIONS TO ASK MENTOR:

1. How is your match (friendship) going so far? How do you feel about being a mentor?

2. Do you and your mentee enjoy spending time together?

3. What kinds of activities do you do when you're together?

4. How do you decide what activities to do together – collaboratively or reciprocally or unilaterally? Do you have trouble thinking up things to do together?

5. Do you spend much time talking together?

6. How often do you see your mentee? How much time do you spend together at each meeting?

7. Does your mentee show up for meetings? Does he/she show up on time or let you know about cancelling in advance?

8. When was your last meeting? What did you do together?

9. Do you talk to your mentee on the telephone? Do you communicate online or using social media? How often?

10. Do you need help with anything? Is there anything interfering with your match (friendship)?

11. How would you describe your mentee's behavior? Does your mentee exhibit any behavior that you don't understand?

12. How are things with your mentee's parents/ guardians and other family members OR teacher at school? Is the parent/ guardian OR teacher cooperative and helpful?

13. Are you satisfied with how things are going? Is there anything that you don't like about the match?

14. Is there any training you think would be helpful? Can we be supportive in any other way?

15. Anything else you'd like to share with me?

QUESTIONS TO ASK MENTEE:

1. How is your match (friendship) going so far?

2. What do you enjoy most about being friends with your mentor?

3. Is there anything that you don't like about the match?

4. What are your favorite activities you did with your mentor this month?

5. Do you remember any activities you didn't like doing?

6. Are there any difficulties or problems in your match (friendship)?

7. Did your mentor help you with any problems you had?

8. When is the last time you saw your mentor?

9. Anything else you'd like to share with me?

QUESTIONS TO ASK PARENT/GUARDIAN:

1.   Is your child happy with his/her mentor?

2.   Does your child look forward to seeing his/her mentor?

3.   Do they seem to enjoy being together?

4.   Is there anything you would like me to discuss with either your child or his/her mentor?

5.   Does your child ever talk to you about his/her mentor? What does he/she say?

6.   How often does your child see his/her mentor? How long do the meetings last?

7.   Does the mentor usually keep appointments and show up on time?

8.   Is there anything that concerns you about the match (friendship)?

9.   Anything else you'd like to share with me?

Adapted from Supporting Mentors: Technical Assistance Packet #6,
Education Northwest/National Mentoring Center

CHAPTER 6:
Informed Intuition

Creating a Portrait

C ompiling data from all available mentor screening tools – from orientation and fingerprinting to interviews, references, training sessions, and interactions – is important in Screening Applicants For Effectiveness. This gathering of objective data, however, is merely the first phase of the screening process. Effective screening is much like creating a "paint-by-number" portrait of each candidate. As a candidate moves through the screening process, colors are added to his or her portrait. There are a vast number of experiences, attitudes, social behaviors, professional activities, interests, emotions, and family dynamics that can be envisioned as tiny sections of the portrait. Attitudes, activities, behaviors, and emotions which are related to any one specific theme would be represented by one color. It is the role of the mentoring staff to paint each section of the picture as the screening process unfolds, ideally leading to a finished portrait. Each "paint-by-number" segment should be filled, the pieces should fit well together, and a rainbow of colors should be present, indicating a healthy balance and a variety of facets to the candidate. If the portrait is incomplete (for example, there is a segment of time that is missing in their lives), is inconsistent (their account of a particular event does not agree with what a reference describes), or is too monochromatic (such as spending an inordinate amount of time socializing with children as opposed to peers), agencies have cause for concern about a candidate's motivation and appropriateness for volunteering with youth.

Informed Intuition

In this "paint-by-number" portrait, the colors of a mentor candidate are drawn from the screening tools but are chosen by a more elusive process. The most critical factor in determining whether or not a candidate should be accepted into your program is Informed Intuition. Intuition is "knowing without knowing why."[104] Informed Intuition is a "gut reaction" to a person, in conjunction with having relevant knowledge. It is vital for agencies to provide child predator training to their staff. This education, together with Informed Intuition, are the most effective tools in screening child predators from youth programs.

There will be times when staff become uncomfortable with a candidate and have a negative "gut reaction" to them. Quite often they "can't put their finger on a specific reason." This intuitive reaction to a candidate may be a first impression, such as during a volunteer recruitment fair or a telephone inquiry. It may also emerge at a later date, such as when a candidate asks inappropriate questions during a training session, when an applicant becomes overly uncomfortable during the interview, or if a reference is reluctant to share information about a candidate. It may even take place after a mentor is matched with a mentee. It is challenging to train staff to use Informed Intuition. "Gut reactions" may seem random and unscientific, and staff are often reluctant to express their negative reactions, fearing that they are being too judgmental.

---

[104] de Becker, Gavin. (1997). *The Gift of Fear*. New York, NY: Dell Publishing. P. 17.

It is extremely difficult for most staff members, especially those who have never dealt with a child predator, to imagine that the candidate with whom they are interacting might be a pedophile. Sometimes staff will explore the reason for their discomfort further, or they may invite another staff person to participate in the interview and ask more probing questions. The danger here is that they might convince themselves that there is no real concern since they will be unable to uncover specific evidence to the contrary.

As an agency, it is important to provide sufficient pedophile training, validate "gut reactions," and empower staff to make judgments based on Informed Intuition. Sergeant Steven McEwan has worked with the Bureau of Investigation's Child Exploitation Unit based in San Jose, California. He states, "I have investigated hundreds of child predator cases involving thousands of victims. In the case of every single victim, there was a woman – the mother, agency staff, a neighbor, a teacher, an aunt – who looked back and said, 'I thought something wasn't right. I had a funny feeling about him.'"[105] Such intuition must be utilized in keeping children safe. "Staff discomfort" must become a sufficient reason to disqualify and reject a candidate. Youth mentoring programs must remember that children, not volunteers, are the clients. An agency's primary responsibility is the safety of children and youth, and staff must therefore always err on the side of caution. Volunteer organizations have the legal right to accept or reject candidates at their discretion. Each program's legal counsel and Board of Directors should develop guidelines for how this is handled. These guidelines must emphasize that every candidate must complete the same application process, no matter who referred them to the program. The final decision regarding their participation in the program must not be influenced by who an applicant knows or their role in the community. And the selection committee's decision must be supported and respected by all agency constituents. Of course, the "screening" process does not end once an applicant is matched in a mentoring relationship. Even utilizing effective screening processes, child molesters may enter into a program, so staff must continue to monitor relationships to ensure the safety and well-being of their mentees.

---

[105] McEwan, Steven. California's San Jose Police Department, Child Exploitation Unit (personal correspondence 2003).

Red Flags

As detailed in Part I of this manual, child molesters are not limited to any one category in terms of socio-economic group, profession, age, gender, ethnicity, educational background, or marital status. While an absolute demographic profile cannot be constructed, research sheds enough information on the motivations, actions, thought processes, and responses of child predators to generate a set of red flags which can be used in the screening process. Red flags are an amalgamation of scientific research, field observations of youth-serving organizations, and law enforcement officials. It is important to remember that no single red flag found within a candidate's life is, by itself, an indicator of a child predator. However, a combination of these indicators should elicit concern on the part of an organization. To effectively use these indicators, screening procedures must be multi-faceted and designed to paint a comprehensive portrait of each candidate's life. Together, Informed Intuition, objective data gathered with mentor screening tools, and red flags offer a process for effectively identifying potential child predators and other inappropriate mentor applicants.

Lack of Balance

Throughout the screening process, programs should evaluate candidates with an emphasis on balance. In order to ensure that an applicant can provide a healthy relationship to a child, they must have a healthy balance to their own lives. They should have a variety of career, social, family, and outside interests. They should have healthy outlets for coping with crises. They should be involved with a number of other individuals in their community. This variety and balance adds color to a candidate's overall portrait; this red flag of a lack of balance may be likened to having a monochromatic "paint-by-number" image. For example, an applicant may present a long list of paid or volunteer experience with youth. On the surface, this individual might seem like an ideal candidate. However, it is important to look critically at this lack of balance to see how these activities fit into the applicant's life. A lack of peer relationships, adult-oriented activities, or other interests and hobbies is a cause for concern. Sometimes this lack of balance may not become apparent until after an individual is matched with a mentee, so staff must continue to assess this aspect of their mentors through ongoing monitoring. This lack of balance may manifest itself as excessive/expensive gift-giving, particularly when not associated with birthdays or holidays. Another example is a mentor's overinvestment in the mentee or including the mentee in every aspect of his or her life.

Extreme Behavior

Extreme or inappropriate behavior is another red flag. Candidates who act outside of the range of expected normal behavior at different stages of the screening process should be scrutinized. Extreme behaviors are often used to control the process or manipulate an applicant's relationship with the program. For example, a candidate may become very impatient with the process and overly anxious to be matched. He or she might say they cannot understand how the process can be so cumbersome: "It's been impossible to volunteer! I just want to help, and it's a major production to go through it!" A candidate may pressure staff to take shortcuts in the screening process. Such candidates are attempting to control the process, deliberately challenging the program boundaries to determine how far they can bend agency rules. They may be assessing whether or not an organization would be a conducive environment to develop an inappropriate relationship with a child. Conversely, a candidate might present staff with an extensive application packet beyond what is requested. This packet might include a separate résumé, employment references, letters of recommendation from friends and family, or copies of certificates and awards.

Candidates might also submit letters from professional therapists, such as a recovering alcoholic who presents an extensive evaluation from a professional who treated him. These applicants may be highly cooperative, submissive, and extremely charming throughout the process: "My life is an open book. If there's anything you want to know, just ask!" This behavior is a manipulative attempt to gain the trust of staff. Whether they are confrontational or overly-accommodating, this extreme behavior may indicate ulterior motives. Extreme behaviors may not be obvious until after an individual is matched with a mentee. Ongoing monitoring allows staff to gauge whether a mentor's reactions are in any way extreme or excessive. For example, a mentor may become overly-focused on documenting his time with his mentee, taking and sharing photographs of the pair's outings and activities, possibly posting them on the Internet. In other cases, a mentor may become overly cooperative or familiar with his program coordinator, frequently stopping by the office to visit. Another red flag would be a mentor who becomes extremely private or secretive about activities with his mentee.

Inappropriate Behavior

Inappropriate behavior may indicate that an applicant is uncomfortable with, conflicted by, or have hidden motives for their involvement with an organization. When asked about how they heard about the program, they may be vague or claim not to remember. Even before they begin the application process, they may be concerned with getting copies of agency brochures, posters, or T-shirts. They may have questions about whether overnight trips are allowed. They may want to know what happens if they are matched with a child who does not like them, or they may express a great deal of concern about the selection process and the odds of being rejected. During the interview, such candidates may not relate to staff in a socially appropriate way. They may be nervous or uncomfortable, act immaturely, giggle, become "shy," change the subject, and go off on tangents. They may express discomfort at what they shared during the interview and write staff afterwards to "clarify certain things that were said." Throughout the screening process, a candidate may make inappropriate remarks or jokes, provide glib answers to questions, or make frequent jokes about being rejected. If asked if they obtained their fingerprints yet, for example, they might respond, "Oh, yeah, my prints are delayed for that kidnapping thing ..." A candidate may ask inappropriate questions during orientation or training sessions, or they may also not relate well to the other adults during these sessions. Such inappropriate behaviors may not be visible until an individual is matched with a mentee. Until the match, staff may not have an opportunity to interact extensively with a mentor, at which time these behaviors may become obvious. A mentor may not behave appropriately at mentor/mentee group activities, for example, or he may show an interest in other mentees at the event. He might also report "suspicious behaviors" by other mentors to staff. This inappropriate behavior may include refusals to comply with a program's guidelines, such as being anxious to have a mentee spend the night, take overnight trips, or spend time camping. Other inappropriate behaviors include excessive physical contact with a mentee (such as tickling, wrestling, or "horse-play") or expressing a strong need to discipline or exercise authority over the mentee.

Over-Involvement with Children

A candidate whose primary life focus is children offers a significant red flag. This extensive involvement with children may be exhibited in a variety of ways. Staff should be concerned by the candidate who is involved in a great many activities that bring him in contact with children, such as teaching, scouting, church youth groups, or youth sports teams. For such a candidate, child-focused activities appear to dominate the applicant's life. Youth involvement might be exhibited by over-identifying with children. During his interaction with a child, a candidate might regress to the child's level of behavior, relinquishing his adult role and responsibility. Such candidates may fail to set limits with the young person, over-indulging the child and allowing him or her to do as they please without constructive supervision or control. Other candidates may become very animated around children. Their eyes might light up, their expressions heighten, and their demeanor could change significantly. Oftentimes, these candidates will contact a mentoring program with a child he is already mentoring informally, asking the program to allow them to officially join the program as a matched pair. References can offer useful information related to these behaviors. A family member might offer feedback: "He loves children! He plays with the children while the rest of the adults are visiting." A longtime family friend might explain that, "He is not afraid to share his feelings with kids. He is a kid himself! He is happiest when he plays with my boys. He is very child-like and gains the confidence of children very easily." Even the candidate may describe himself as qualified because, "I love seeing kids happy. It makes me forget about my troubles ... I am a magnet for children, and I want to share myself with someone." Or, "I'm crazy about kids: I love to spend time with them ... I speak their language ... I never get bored being with them." This over-involvement with children may not become fully apparent before the match, so ongoing monitoring is vital as staff continue to gain knowledge about their mentors. One example of this is a mentor who, once matched, begins to involve other boys on outings with his mentee, particularly young people not known to the mentee, not related to the mentor or mentee, and not connected to program. Another example is a mentor who may not want to leave town to accept another job because he does not want to leave his mentee. Over-involvement may also be seen as a mentor getting into "childish" arguments with his mentee, acting at the mentee's level, or exhibiting an inability to set limits or provide constructive supervision for the mentee.

Under-Involvement with Adults

Just as over-involvement with children is a concern, so is under-involvement with adults. This component, however, may be challenging to uncover. Child predators adapt to a society that does not share their views, and they are tremendously adept at masking their feelings and beliefs. They will ingratiate themselves with other adults and accepted community institutions and are often perceived as true champions of youth and community service. A closer examination of their adult relationships, however, may reveal that these are only superficial connections. A closer examination of their social circles may reveal inconsistencies. For example, a candidate may show character immaturity with in-depth adult interactions, such as by being extremely shy, withdrawn, passive, or nonassertive. He may indicate anxiety regarding adult sexuality, may have an abnormal sexual development history, or may lack adult dating experiences or relationships. The absence of appropriate peer relationships is a red flag, particularly if the candidate's circle of friends is confined to significantly younger associates. The candidate may rarely have meaningful relationships with other adults in their non-work hours. He may have difficulty providing references, or his references may not be able to provide much personal information about the candidate or may not have known him for long. A lack of true adult relationships provides staff with a significant red flag indicator. Staff should also continue to watch for this under-involvement with adults after the match. Like many of these red flags, these indicators may not become apparent during the pre-match screening period.

Focus on Personal Needs

A candidate might express preferences during the matching process. He might describe his desired match very specifically, including age, physical characteristics, emotional demeanor, ethnicity, or being matched with an only child. For example, they might state, "I'm flexible, but I would have more in common with an underprivileged Caucasian child between 10 and 12 years old, fairly fit and active, real open, willing to learn and try things." A candidate might specify wanting a "clean" or "well-groomed" child. Often, such a candidate will request a program's "neediest" child, a young person that "no one wants," or a mentee with the "worst" parents. During the application process, such a candidate might express worry about what would happen if he and the mentee did not "get along."

Again, references can offer useful comments, such as, "I don't know how he'd do if there was no chemistry between him and the young person." Or, "This is a good program for him because he would make a good friend, but he would also benefit because he is looking for direction right now and needs friends." Throughout the application process, staff will encounter indicators of whether a candidate has specific needs that may be inappropriate. Even after the match, staff must continue ongoing monitoring since this focus on personal needs may not be obvious before an individual is matched with his or her mentee. It may not become apparent, for example, until the mentor's needs are somehow not being met and he suddenly wants to terminate his match without a specified reason. Another example would be a mentor who reveals that he is going through a stressful time in his life then begins to use his mentee as a confidant or primary support system. Staff should also take note if a mentee is too often included in a mentor's adult activities (particularly during evening hours) at which the mentee assumes the role of the mentor's "date" or companion during events at which most adults would interact with their same-age peers.

Unhealthy Attitudes

Both directly and indirectly, candidates provide information regarding their attitudes which staff can use to identify potential child predators. Attitudinal red flags include strong views on children and youth – which a candidate may express passionately. Such candidates may stress that children should be treated as equals to adults. They often believe that children should be given the love that they need, be given the chance to experience and enjoy real companionship, and be allowed to make their own decisions in regard to traditionally-adult behaviors such as pleasure and sex. Such a candidate may express a revulsion or extremely judgmental attitude toward homosexuality. He may say that he is sickened by child abuse and understands why children are scared to tell anyone when it occurs. Candidates may be indignant that society will not let men hug boys more. A candidate might want to teach sex education to a young person, stating that he would have appreciated knowing more about sex when he was young. Such attitudes are common child predator red flags which can support staff in helping to protect their mentees. Even after the match, it is important to continue the "screening" process through ongoing monitoring since a mentor's unhealthy attitudes may not become apparent until he is matched with a mentee. For example, a mentor may attempt to push the boundaries of the relationship through a specific issue, such as cleanliness. This mentor might explain that his mentee (or his mentee's home) is unclean, so he may begin the pair's weekly outings by having the mentee take a shower or wash his clothes at the mentor's home. This could lead to opportunities for the mentor to teach his mentee about "proper hygiene" or to other related discussions. In another example, a mentor may make "reports" about problems with his child's family or about other mentoring relationships, then attempt to involve mentoring program staff in this manufactured situation. By continuing to monitor mentors and watch for red flag indicators, alert staff can quickly identify such unhealthy attitudes and problematic behaviors.

Problematic Personal Interests

Some hobbies and interests are potential red flags. For example, when asked about interests and how they would spend time with a child, a candidate may provide vague, non-specific answers:

- "I do lots of things."
- "I like to just hang out."
- "Driving around and sightseeing."
- "Visiting friends."
- "Day trips."
- "Watching movies at home."

Other areas of concern include a very strong interest in long-term, unsupervised activities. This might include camping, hunting, fishing, hiking or backpacking, or a day at the beach. A candidate might also talk about spending time in a vacation home or with friends and family outside of your community. Another potential red flag is an interest in photography or video-production. These personal interests might not be identified until after the match has been made, so staff must continue to monitor the activities of the mentor/mentee pair. For example, a mentee might complain about too much sedentary time, such as spending time in front of the television or "just hanging out" at the mentor's apartment.

Problematic Background Indicators

There are many background indicators that have been identified as highly-correlated to child predator activities. Again, this is not to say that individuals who fit into one or more of these categories are child predators. These are simply red flags which, if present in conjunction with other factors (such as discrepancies in information collected or extremes in attitudes and behaviors), should be considered in your candidate assessment. Like all red flags, these may not be uncovered or become apparent until after an individual is matched with a mentee. Ongoing monitoring of mentors, therefore, is crucial to protecting mentees. This should be conducted in conjunction with ongoing mentee monitoring and family communication to identify indicators such as parental discomfort with the mentor or rapid/significant changes in a mentee's school performance or behaviors at home. Some problematic mentor background indicators include

- A candidate who has a history of being abused, neglected, or sexually victimized. Sometimes a candidate will not state this fact, but he may allude to a teacher or family member with whom there seemed to be a negative relationship. He may also mention other family members who were abused or give vague answers when asked if he was ever the victim of abuse ("I don't think so, but I have no strong memories ..." or "It depends on your definition of abuse."). It is critical not to victimize the victim again: the great majority of individuals who have been abused do not become abusers. However, the majority of child molesters were abused as children.
- A candidate with a police record, even if it is seemingly unrelated to crimes against children.
- A candidate or a candidate whose parents or close family members have or had a history of alcohol abuse or regular alcohol or drug use.
- A candidate with a history of depression.
- A candidate who is still seeing children that he or she met through other programs. The candidate might say that they are interested in finding another child who can help relate to that child.
- A history of moving from job to job or place to place.
- A job which requires moving or traveling from place to place, particularly overseas.
- A candidate who lives far from a program's service area. Their explanation might be that, "I spend a lot of time in this community" or "There aren't any good programs like yours in my community."
- A candidate who has held many lower-echelon jobs with no ambition for responsibility or advancement. This candidate might exhibit avoidance of decision-making positions.

- A candidate who was referred by another youth-serving agency. Unfortunately, some programs turn applicants down by referring them to other organizations.
- A candidate who has applied to a similar program or has participated in other programs but was not satisfied with these organizations: "They weren't very organized. I am certain that your program will be much better and much more accommodating."
- A candidate with an interest in photography.
- A candidate with an interest in aviation and travel, particularly to impoverished countries.

It is important to have a multi-faceted approach to screening, both before and after a candidate is matched with a mentee. Red flags may be immediately obvious, they may slowly become apparent, or they may be reflected in sudden unexplained changes within a mentoring relationship. Each screening step provides key information to effectively assess whether a candidate would be an appropriate mentor, helping to create a complete "paint-by-number" portrait of a candidate. And the most critical factor in determining whether or not an applicant may be a child predator is Informed Intuition, combining staff education, objective data, and a "gut reaction" to a particular candidate.

Creating a Customized Inventory

It is important to maintain the confidentiality of your files and protect the identities of the children, youth, mentors, and mentor candidates you encounter over time. These files can, however, become a valuable resource in your agency's learning protocol around keeping your mentees safe from harm. By conducting periodic assessments of mentors who were turned down for potential safety reasons, you can create an inventory of characteristics, behaviors, interests, and other volunteer application circumstances. You may be surprised at the number of elements that you find in common among these applicants. No factor is too trivial or seemingly irrelevant to overlook. For example, you might find that camping is a common pastime. Does this mean that anyone with camping as a hobby is a child predator? Of course not. However, child predators might use camping as a way to isolate a child, so you can add this to your list of red flags when you screen candidates.

CHAPTER 7:
Hypothetical Situations

The following hypothetical situations were created to illustrate the process of gathering objective data, using mentor screening tools, applying Informed Intuition, and exploring red flags. The agency actions from each scenario are fictional. The characters, while also fictional, are based on both common and uncommon mentor applicants who have applied to Friends for Youth, Inc., and other mentoring programs, with details modified to ensure confidentiality.

Case A: Albert

Stephanie, the recruitment coordinator, spoke with him on the telephone. Despite her assurance that all topics would be covered at the orientation, he had a range of questions about The Agency, the mentees, and the application process. At the end of the conversation, she signed him up for the next orientation session, scheduled for that weekend. Albert arrived on time for his orientation. He was extremely friendly with the other applicants, as well as with Jesse, the staff person conducting the session. The orientation session covered The Agency's mission, goals, the tremendous needs of at-risk youth, and types of youth served by the program. Albert asked a number of questions about the application process and the typical problems of the mentees' families. At the end of the session, Albert signed up for an interview. Gertie visited Albert's home for the interview early the next week.

Although his application form was not yet complete, Albert assured her that he would mail it shortly. During the interview, Gertie discussed Albert's interest in the program, his current time commitments and work schedule, work history, and personal interests. Albert, age 35, said that he had been raised by a single mother, without many male role models. He wanted to be that role model for youth in his community. He had enjoyed his previous volunteer activities, such as coaching both baseball and swimming at the YMCA in his old neighborhood. When he moved to the area six months ago, he had found work through a local education program which offered tutoring to middle and high school students. He had done this type of work before, and he enjoyed the independence and flexible schedule. Albert's hobbies ranged from hiking and camping to interactive online gaming and digital photography. Because he had moved so recently, he did not have any personal references who were local. He did provide four contacts: his landlady, his current boss, his previous boss, and a coworker from his previous tutoring employer. After the interview, Gertie contacted his references who all recommended him as being enthusiastic about his volunteer projects. Overall, Gertie found Albert to be friendly, but she did not feel particularly comfortable with him. Albert brought his application to the volunteer training a week later. During the training, Albert seemed engaged in all of the material, particularly the "scenarios" exercise when he seemed somewhat concerned about parental involvement. Albert's fingerprints and driving record arrived soon after the training, and he was matched the following week with 10-year-old Joshua. Unfortunately, Joshua's interest in the program waned after about two months. When Gertie called Joshua's mother, she said that she was not sure that Albert was the right mentor for Joshua. Gertie knew she was somewhat protective of Joshua, so she was not surprised when Joshua's mom said she really did not like the activities they had been doing which took Joshua out of the house for a whole day at a time. Joshua's mom said that she was going to find a different program for her son. Gertie called Albert to tell him that The Agency would find another mentee for him.

Red Flags and Informed Intuition

A written description can be easy to second-guess, but assume that this is a full picture of the information available about Albert. This scenario includes a significant number of red flags. First, Albert is apparently a single male in his mid-thirties who makes no mention of whether he has/had a partner or is/was dating. He seems to have no circle of friends, despite the fact that he is friendly with staff and other volunteer applicants. His type of work is a concern, particularly since his tutoring –like his volunteer activities – offers long periods of unsupervised time with youth. Albert's hobbies are somewhat of a concern. His short length of time in the area, combined with a lack of personal references, offers another red flag. Even the comments of the references are a problem: they note only his enthusiasm with volunteer projects without mention of any interests, characteristics, or even a description of "that afternoon we all went to the ball game together." His specific interest in the problems of mentee families and parental involvement is a potential indicator. In hindsight, Joshua's reaction and the comments of his mother should have been indicators about issues with Albert's role as a mentor.

Agency Shortfalls

Although many of the mentor screening mechanisms are in place, The Agency did not appropriately utilize these tools. First, the orientation material did not highlight the screening process and the ongoing monitoring of mentor/mentee pairs. For child predators, such details often results in their lack of follow-through when they recognize that a relationship would take place WITHIN the agency and WITH agency involvement. Next, Albert did not submit his application before or (at the very least) during the interview. This is an important tool for staff, allowing the interviewer to ask questions about missing, inconsistent, or unusual information. The interview itself did not fully explore important questions about Albert: What was his childhood like? Is he single, divorced, or dating? Where are his mother and other family members, and is he in touch with them? Why or why not? What other types of jobs has he held? Does he have other friends? Why did he move to the area? Albert's short length of time in the area and his fairly quick completion of the application process should have been issues of concern as well. More importantly, The Agency did not utilize its most important screening tool, its staff. The Agency did not have any mechanism in place for staff to share their concerns or utilize their informed intuition during the screening process. Stephanie could have alerted Jesse about Albert's enthusiasm and refusal to wait for the orientation to discuss program details. Jesse could have mentioned Albert's unusual questions about mentee families, alerting Gertie to an issue which could have been explored at the interview, through references, or during the training. Gertie could also have shared with staff her discomfort with Albert. Even after matching him with Joshua, The Agency should have had a detailed process for reviewing closed relationships, parent feedback, and direct child feedback. Albert's day-long activities would have been part of this review, as well as other information from the monitoring notes, had the agency been in regular contact with Joshua, his mom, or Albert. Gertie was premature in telling Albert that The Agency would find another mentee for him.

Did You Know?

Background checks: A "clean" background report based on fingerprints or the Megan's Law Database does not necessarily mean that an applicant is safe to be matched with a child. This only means that the applicant has not yet been convicted of child molestation. Experts estimate that only a small percentage of child predators have been identified, often after molesting a multitude of victims. Additionally, there are errors and inaccuracies with background checks, so they should not be used as a sole determining factor in mentor screening.

Molester Resources: NAMBLA (North American Man Boy Love Association) and similar groups are highly organized. These groups promote man/boy and adult/child relationships and provide resources to help child predators successfully infiltrate youth organizations. Such resources may include "correct" interview responses, how to behave with youth agency staff, and how to choose an agency which does not thoroughly screen or regularly monitor adult/youth relationships. Through the Internet, these groups even link child predators to the websites of agencies which may offer easy access to children.

Conclusion

Albert has too many red flags to have been matched with Joshua, let alone another child. This applicant had too many missing pieces of information with too few adult relationships and too many youth-oriented activities. In addition, staff intuition may likely have raised additional questions, had staff been properly trained and feedback mechanisms been in place. Albert too closely fits the profile of a child predator to allow his interaction with any of The Agency's mentees.

Case B: Ben

Ben found out about The Agency through a lunchtime presentation at his workplace. He was extremely engaged in the presentation and immediately requested additional information. Dawn, a program coordinator, gave him directions to The Agency with the date and time of the next orientation. Ben arrived 20 minutes early for the orientation. He asked a number of questions during the orientation, particularly regarding the needs of the mentees and how the program referrals were made. After the orientation, Dawn spoke with Genevieve, the program coordinator who would be conducting Ben's interview. She shared that Ben seemed particularly enthusiastic, but he had not asked any inappropriate questions or exhibit behaviors which made her uncomfortable. Ben's application arrived a week later, several days before his interview. The application information was sparse and with some blank answer spaces, but he did provide four references (two coworkers, his boss, and his elderly aunt, with whom he shared a house). During the interview, Genevieve found 27-year-old Ben particularly friendly and engaging. His responses helped to fill in the details missing from his application, with one exception. When asked about his dating history, he was visibly uncomfortable. When pressed for information, he provided a brief response and changed the direction of the conversation. Ben had lived in the area for most of his life, and his hobbies included backpacking, surfing the Web, and watching movies. After the interview, Genevieve spoke with The Agency's volunteer trainer, Jack. She explained that there was clearly something that Ben was withholding, but she was not uncomfortable talking with him. During the training, Jack was conscious of Ben's ability to participate in the group discussions, and no negative issues presented themselves. Ben's fingerprints and clean driving record arrived shortly afterwards. Dawn, Genevieve, and Jack discussed Ben's application at their next staff meeting. Although there were a number of red flags on his application, the team chose to complete the process before making a decision on his application. Ben called two weeks later to see how the process was going. Genevieve let him know that the process was not complete because she was having difficulty contacting his references. She finally reached his boss who spoke highly of his work ethic and his willingness to help others during times of heavy work schedules. Genevieve had not met Ben's aunt during the home visit, but she finally reached Aunt Ellie. Ellie answered each of the questions very carefully, telling Genevieve what a nice young man Ben had always been. "I'm so glad that he's finally doing better," commented Aunt Ellie. Genevieve asked, "Doing better?" "Since the accident," responded Aunt Ellie. She explained that Ben had been in a terrible auto accident right after college. His childhood sweetheart had also been in the car and was killed. Even though the accident was caused by a tire blow-out, Ben had always blamed himself. He had finally started therapy a year ago, and he had come to live with his aunt to give him a change of scenery. Genevieve eventually reached his coworkers. Both went backpacking regularly with Ben, and one had attended a film festival with him earlier in the fall.

Red Flags and Informed Intuition

Initially, Ben exhibited a number of potential red flags. The fact that he was nearly 30 years old and living with a family member was somewhat questionable. His incomplete application and avoidance of specific personal questions was a concern, as were some of his orientation questions. His seemingly solitary hobbies also presented potential concerns. The Agency staff had been trained to look for red flags and to talk to each other about concerns. Although they were all somewhat worried about certain aspects of his application, none of them had an uncomfortable feeling about Ben. Ben's profile had seemed incomplete but not inconsistent. While they were careful not to dismiss their concerns, The Agency's team utilized all aspects of the mentor screening process and eventually completed Ben's application "portrait."

Agency Shortfalls

Based on the scenario information provided, Ben did not withhold information – The Agency's interview process had just not asked the right questions. If the interview included questions about any major injuries, any traumatic losses in his life, or had an open-ended question regarding other life events or challenges, Ben may have disclosed this piece of information. Had he been asked whether he had ever been in counseling or seen a therapist, some of the staff's concerns could also have been answered earlier. As it was posed, The Agency's "dating history" question clearly did not generate the needed information. If they had grown up together, Ben may not have considered time spent with his "childhood sweetheart" to be "dating." It is possible that Ben's awkward response was based on his lack of success in dating after the car accident, a question which may have been more uncomfortable if he found Genevieve attractive. At this point, The Agency has a dilemma. Because references responses are confidential, Genevieve cannot simply call Ben and ask about the accident. One option would be to tell Ben that – although a final decision about his application had not yet been made –

The Agency had received a number of recent referrals of children with a range of needs. In trying to find the best mentor for some of these young people, Genevieve could explain that she had some follow-up questions related to his attitudes toward and experience with counseling and loss. This would allow an opportunity for Ben to share useful information. His responses could help fill in pieces of his overall profile, as well as determine whether he was emotionally ready to be a mentor. Not asking the right questions will often result in not receiving the right answers. Luckily, the team did use their intuition to recognize that they did not yet have a complete picture of Ben.

Did You Know?

Training: Various resources exist to help agencies properly train their staff on how to screen for mentors. Many of these resources are listed in Part III of this volume. The most useful tools, however, are those within an agency: programs should plan for sufficient training time, allowing new staff opportunities to observe coworkers, practice during mock interviews, then be shadowed by more experienced staff members. In addition to educational programs, this experiential learning helps ensure that staff members are familiar with the agency's unique processes, as well as the steps needed to screen for child predators. Because of the crucial role of the direct services staff, this process should not be rushed, minimized, or omitted.

Conclusion

Ben's red flags were actually indicators that a major piece of information was missing. Depending on his response and openness to the question about counseling, Ben could bring unique understanding to a mentee who had experienced loss or was receiving counseling support. Without the staff's informed intuition, they might have eliminated Ben as a mentor or they might have accepted him without recognizing a crucial piece of data.

Case C: Calvin

Pat, The Agency's newest Board member, met Calvin several years ago through a mixer at the local Chamber of Commerce, and they had since done some business together. Calvin owned real estate in the area and had many connections that could benefit The Agency's fundraising efforts. Upon joining the Board, Pat put the program coordinators in touch with Calvin because he sounded interested in becoming a mentor. Sue, a program coordinator, called Calvin to invite him to come to the next orientation. Donald was the staff person conducting the orientation. This was one of the first orientation sessions that Donald would be conducting since being hired two months earlier. Donald thought Calvin was a real "go-getter," and he found Calvin enthusiastic about helping such "troubled" youth. After the orientation, Calvin signed up for an interview. Despite his busy schedule, he made time for the interview to occur a few days after the orientation. His availability for the interview again happened to fall onto Donald's schedule. Calvin delivered his application to the office the day after the orientation so that Donald would have it before the interview. Donald reviewed the application and set out for the interview. Calvin lived in a gated community in a very nice neighborhood. Now in his early forties, he had been married briefly ("in a moment of weakness, ha-ha!") but had been divorced for about 15 years. He had lived in the area most of his life, and he felt that his financial success obligated him to help others. He sat on a number of local nonprofit boards and was extremely active in his church's youth group. He told Donald that he had applied to another mentoring organization, but they seemed to be very disorganized and had not followed up with his application. Calvin was also happy to help with some group activities: he had been a pilot for Eastern Airlines and still had some friends at the airport who could help arrange a tour for the mentors and mentees. Because Sue, The Agency's other program coordinator, was now on vacation, Donald was conducting the next volunteer training. Calvin was eager to complete the process and signed up for the training. Calvin was the "class clown" of the training session. Donald thought that Calvin added a touch of humor to the session, even though he seemed to make a few too many jokes while Donald covered material on the Mentor Code of Conduct. After the training, Donald began working on his references. Although he had known Board member Pat and the other three individuals for many years, none provided more than a cursory description of Calvin. Even Pat was actually only an business acquaintance. The final items needed to complete the application were a driving record and fingerprint record. On Monday, Calvin called to see if these items had arrived. Donald apologized and said they had not. Calvin called again the following Monday, as well as during the following two weeks. Each time, Calvin seemed more and more aggravated about the delay. Pat also called Donald to ask why the process seemed to be taking so long. When Donald's driving record finally arrived, he decided to match Calvin and complete the file with the fingerprints when they arrived. Donald matched Calvin with

Miguel, a 12-year old living with his mother and several younger sisters. After about a month, Calvin called to say that his match was not working. Miguel was not opening up to him, and Miguel had too much energy to sit still for some of the activities that Calvin planned. Besides, Miguel did not seem to have enough "problems" to really need a mentor. Calvin asked whether there might be a "needier" child, perhaps one who was younger and quieter. While waiting to re-match Calvin, a letter arrived stating that his fingerprint check had been delayed for 45 days.

Red Flags and Informed Intuition

From the start, Calvin's extreme behavior should have provided a red flag for staff members. His particular interest in the most "needy" and "troubled" children also presented a problem. Having been a pilot, Calvin falls into a demographic with an increased number of child predators, and this should have provided another issue of concern for staff. Another red flag was Calvin's comments regarding the other mentoring agency which had not followed up on his application: the truth of this statement would be worth pursuing. Based on the information provided in this hypothetical situation, Calvin appears to have too few genuine relationships with adults and many involvements (such as through the youth group) with youth. For having such a busy schedule, Calvin seemed overly-helpful in dropping off his application material, making time to immediately attend an orientation and training, and offering to coordinate group activities. His behavior after being matched with Miguel is equally troublesome: while the program is designed to address the needs of mentees, Calvin seems more concerned with having his own needs met. It is unclear whether The Agency had trained Donald on the use of red flags or Informed Intuition, but his relatively short period of time in his role may have hindered The Agency's ability to effectively screen volunteers.

Agency Shortfalls

All individuals involved with The Agency – including Board members – should be educated on the importance of proper volunteer screening. As part of their own training, Board members should fully understand the volunteer application process and agree to abide by the judgment of the staff and selection committee members involved in the screening and final decision. The Agency's first shortfall was in failing to ensure that Pat understand that the role of a Board member to recruit supporters and volunteers ended when Calvin was put in touch with the staff. Another major problem with the presented scenario is that Donald was the only staff member to spend any length of time with Calvin. Without meeting additional staff, The Agency could not benefit from another perspective. It is possible that Sue would not have found Calvin enthusiastic and funny but pushy and inappropriate. The Agency's own records may have offered an additional tool: given that he had lived in the area for many years, it is somewhat unusual that Calvin had not investigated this volunteer opportunity until he had a direct connection to the agency through Pat. If it has been in existence for any length of time, it might be useful for The Agency to check its records to see whether Calvin had, in fact, previously applied to the program. Also, The Agency should have followed up with the other mentoring organization which Calvin described as "disorganized." It is possible that the other program would not have been able to confirm whether or not Calvin had applied to their program. Many programs, however, are willing to speak "off the record" for the sake of the safety of children. Even if they were only able to confirm that Calvin had applied, that his file had been closed, and that they had no plans to match him, this level of detail would have assisted staff in confirming problematic issues with his application. Based on the information provided, The Agency also fell short by not conducting a Sexual Offender Registry check. Under no condition should Calvin have been matched without his full background check having been completed.

Did You Know?

Fingerprint Delays: Fingerprint background checks can be delayed for a number of reasons. Although no government official can explain why a specific individual's prints are being delayed, agency staff can ask for the types of issues which might cause a delay. According to phone conversations with representatives from the Department of Justice, prints are sometimes delayed because of an internal processing problem at the fingerprint office. The fingerprint record may be unreadable, and a "re-print" request may be forthcoming. The applicant may have a common name or may share a name with someone who has a criminal record. Or, the applicant may have a criminal record, but the Department of Justice must determine whether to report that criminal offense, depending on whether it is related to the type of background check being requested by an agency.

Conclusion

Calvin should not have been matched, and he should not be re-matched. The primary duty of youth service providers is caring for the well-being, healthy development, and growth of children. Even when it appears that a mentor may potentially become disinterested during his or her wait to be matched, it is vital to complete the application and screening process, utilize all available mentor screening tools, address red flags, and value staff's Informed Intuition. There is no acceptable "margin of error."

Case D: Deenie

Deenie emailed The Agency following a recruitment effort which placed advertisements on the back of grocery store receipts. She received details for and attended the next orientation session at the office. The orientation covered profiles of mentees, The Agency's tremendous need for mentors, and an invitation to sign up for an interview. When The Agency's staff met for their weekly Team Meeting, Rosa, who conducted the orientation, described Deenie as polite and quiet. Rosa was assigned to conduct Deenie's interview, and she carefully reviewed the application when it arrived a week later. Deenie's application form had several topics which would warrant follow-up: Deenie had an unspecified university degree, and there was no work history for almost seven years after her graduation from college. During the interview, Rosa felt that Deenie was more stand-offish than shy. All of Deenie's answers were extremely direct and specific. As a woman in her early-thirties, Rosa felt Deenie had few interests (reading and following the National Basketball Association) and a very small circle of acquaintances, particularly for being a clerk in a large department store at the local mall. Rosa asked Deenie about her college experience, as well as her studies and degree. Deenie was fairly vague about her general studies, stating that she ended up with mathematics degree. In trying to lighten Deenie's mood and draw out additional information, Rosa joked that, "As an English major, my family often asked what I planned to do with my degree … teach? What about you?" Without smiling, Deenie responded that she had planned on teaching, but that plan did not work out. Through the interview, Rosa also found out that Deenie was not close with her parents or brother, and she had been married to basketball player she met in college but was now divorced. Near the end of the interview, Rosa asked whether she might be willing to be matched with either a girl or a boy since The Agency did periodically consider female mentor/male mentee matches. Deenie said yes. Rosa then told Deenie she would begin working on her references and gave her a list of remaining items for Deenie to complete for her application: driving record, proof of insurance, fingerprinting, and volunteer training. Rosa soon began work on Deenie's references. She contacted her current supervisor and two coworkers, all of whom had positive but superficial comments to make about the short period of time they had known her. The final person on Deenie's reference list was an older cousin who lived quite far away and two time zones ahead. Rosa tried unsuccessfully to contact Deenie to see if she might be able to help with the contact. Rosa finally received an early-morning voice message from Deenie's cousin saying that Deenie was "a very positive person who would be a great role model to some young lady." Rosa continued to try to contact the cousin directly, and she also begin trying to contact Deenie. After several weeks without any contact from Deenie, Rosa sent her The Agency's standardized letter which thanked Deenie for her interest and explained that her information would be closed but kept on file until Deenie again contacted the agency.

Red Flags and Informed Intuition

Rosa's experience of Deenie as stand-offish was one of the telling items of this scenario: Rosa was recognizing Deenie's discomfort with some aspect of the program or the screening process. The vague information about her college and early work experience was an important issue to recognize, and the continued disconnect of this information during the interview confirms problematic aspects to the topic. Did Deenie become a teacher? Was she dismissed for some reason? If she were interested in teaching, why has she apparently had no interactions with youth? Did her marriage fail at the same time that her teaching career "did not work out?" Are these issues related? There is also little explanation for why Deenie has little contact with her family, why her marriage might have failed, and why a distant cousin was provided as a reference. Deenie's material includes far too many questions for her to be considered a mentor candidate at this time, and her self-selection to discontinue the process confirms that staff was likely to reject her application.

Agency Shortfalls

From the description, it appears that the full list of background check steps was not presented during The Agency's orientation. It is possible that Deenie recognized that one of the final items (likely the driving record or fingerprinting) would have resulted in a disqualification. If Deenie had been told of these steps from the beginning, she may not have signed up for an interview, particularly if she had a criminal record preventing her from having contact with youth. Some of The Agency's Interview questions might benefit from review, particularly regarding follow-up to the issues Deenie failed to disclose, such as a more detailed family history and marital history. In terms of volunteer recruitment, broad-based campaigns do reach a wider portion of the population, but these efforts sometimes result in a larger number of inappropriate candidates seeking details about volunteering. For example, grocery store receipt campaigns, a recruitment table at an art and wine festival, or the pre-movie slide show advertisements do increase visibility – just not always to the most ideal or appropriate potential mentors. When implementing any recruitment effort, staff should identify and be prepared for the queries these campaigns may generate.

Did You Know?

Hidden Details: Unless presented by an applicant, many pieces of information are extremely difficult to uncover. Even if involved in a serious crime, a candidate's legal issues may have been settled through a plea bargain or have gained little publicity. Without fingerprint checks, even the most high-profile case may be hidden by a candidate through name changes, careful selection of references, or selective disclosure of background information.

Conclusion

At the least, Deenie has a personal issue which made her an inappropriate mentor candidate. It is also possible that her background included more serious issues which would pose a threat to the safety of a child. In addition to a significant number of red flags, Deenie's incomplete application disqualifies her from becoming a mentor, and her name and file should be carefully documented in case she applies to The Agency at a later date.

Case E: Edwin

Edwin contacted The Agency after finding the volunteer opportunity listing on the Internet. He was scheduled to attend an orientation and arrived at an appropriate time. Shanika conducted the orientation. She had little interaction with Edwin, but her observations were that he was very attentive and enthusiastic. During her orientation report to her coworkers, she stated that Edwin asked several questions regarding the needs of the mentees, the family issues of a typical mentee, and whether most mentees and mentors meet for at least the program's initial one-year period. Shanika was also scheduled to conduct Edwin's interview, so she carefully reviewed his written application. Edwin's responses were brief but complete, and Shanika was hopeful that his experience as a parent might fit well for the children in the program. On the night of the interview, Shanika arrived at the house expecting to meet Edwin's family. He explained that his wife and two boys might be back by the end of the interview, but that the family rarely spent much time together until the evenings because of their busy schedules. During the interview, Shanika learned that Edwin had grown up in the area and had had a difficult childhood: his father left when he was a baby, and his mother struggled to provide for him. Her boyfriend moved into their apartment when he was in elementary school, but the boyfriend was physically abusive toward Edwin's mother, a topic Edwin apparently found difficult to share with Shanika. Edwin said he had focused on school and sports, eventually finishing high school and joining the Army for four years. He then returned to the area, attended college, and started a small business. His company and his investments did particularly well, and he began looking for ways to give back to the community. He volunteered through several youth organizations, and during one such volunteer project he met his wife, Glenda. She had two boys involved with the youth program, and Edwin met her when she came to pick them up at the end of a camping trip he had chaperoned. Glenda had been a single parent for many years. She and her boys (Marcus, then eight years old, and Philip, then nine) were struggling financially, forcing Glenda to work several jobs. Edwin had told Glenda to call if she ever needed help bringing them home after program activities. Glenda did call, and Edwin explained that he fell in love with her and the whole family. Edwin said that Marcus and Philip are now very involved in high school activities, so he does not see them much, but he is excited that they are both doing well and planning to head off to college in the near future. As Shanika and Edwin finished the interview, Glenda and the boys returned home. The boys were very polite ("Hello, ma'am.") when introduced, then quickly headed to another part of the house. Glenda offered a similar brief greeting before leaving the room. Before the interview, Shanika had noticed that Edwin had not included his wife as a reference, so Shanika mentioned that she would like to talk to Glenda as well – "a typical practice for applicants who are married or in a relationship, just to make sure that they are comfortable with their partner's involvement in the program." In actuality, Shanika had not previously had a husband not include their wife as a reference, so her statement was inherently true. Edwin seemed surprised and said that he could see if she was available right now, but Shanika (wanting to speak with Glenda alone) said she would call Glenda later since she did not have the reference questions with her. After the interview, Shanika completed her notes and was concerned by the combination of some details from Edwin's interview. She had also felt very uncomfortable with Edwin throughout the interview, a fact she noted in her evaluation. Because she was supposed to conduct the next volunteer training, she called to offer Edwin two of the other upcoming training dates. Wanting to further explore some of the disconcerting aspects of the interview, Shanika chose to complete the reference checks herself. The references were all prominent business owners and community members, so they were difficult to contact and had little time to complete the reference check. All four had known Edwin for a number of years, but none had spent time with him and his family socially. They each seemed to have had fairly superficial interactions with Edwin. Two of the references commented on what a great mentor he would be, caring so much for the welfare of children: "Edwin was so wonderful to Glenda and the boys. He saved them from poverty and provided them with a big, beautiful home and private schools." Shanika also finally spoke with Glenda as well. Glenda did not have much to say, and Shanika found her to be painfully timid. She answered all of Shanika's questions, but her responses were not particularly enlightening and sounded somewhat rehearsed. After the volunteer training, Shanika's coworker, Beverly, reported that Edwin had been an average participant. Because of the number of attendees and Shanika's request to pay particular attention to Edwin, Beverly had paired herself with Edwin during one of the one-on-one discussion activities. She said that she found Edwin "odd" but enthusiastic about the prospect of becoming a mentor. After completing all of the steps of the application process, Edwin was not accepted as a mentor.

Red Flags and Informed Intuition

This agency trained their staff regularly on effective screening procedures. While no one aspect indicates a child predator, Shanika recognized that Edwin's history contained a number of factors frequently connected with child predator profiles, particularly his personal history and the way in which he integrated himself into Glenda's family. Shanika was extremely aware that Edwin was applying to become a mentor just as his stepsons were becoming young men. Edwin's seeming lack of adult relationships was also a concern. Most importantly, however, was Shanika's "gut reaction." Even if Beverly had not found Edwin to be "odd" and even if Shanika had somehow reconciled a few of Edwin's red flag issues, the fact remained that she was very uncomfortable with him. Shanika's training in child safety prepared her to recognize her feelings and not try to rationalize her doubts.

Agency Shortfalls

The Agency did not have any shortfalls related to Edwin's application to the program. The staff were careful to follow all of the required steps in the process, gathering objective data and carefully documenting all communication. By following its procedures and validating staff intuition, The Agency very possibly avoided placing a child in contact with an adult who might harm him. Barring a rejected applicant's future conviction for harming a child, organizations seldom receive confirmation that their rejection was justified. This is, unfortunately, a challenge for mentoring programs, but such suspicion is warranted when the welfare of a child is at stake. Because it is better to reject an appropriate volunteer than risk pairing a mentee with a child predator, The Agency succeeded in doing their best to provide safe, quality mentoring services.

Did You Know?

Creating a Rejection History: No single factor is an indicator of a child molester, but a combination of red flags and staff intuition provides the best protection against placing a mentee in danger. Because every community and program is unique, agencies will benefit from the practice of documenting cases in which they reject an applicant. This same practice should be applied for mentors who are matched but whose relationships or personal interactions with staff prove problematic. By developing this type of historical record, agencies can use this information to train new mentoring staff and track any regional trends related to volunteer applicants who may be child predators. Agencies should seek the assistance of their legal counsel on how to best document, record, and file such information. Additionally, agencies should build relationships with local law enforcement organizations, who may have further guidance on steps that can be taken to protect children in the community.

Conclusion

Edwin's rejection letter was sent to his home. He did not contact the agency following receipt of his rejection letter. His information was filed according to agency policies, based on advice of The Agency's legal counsel for recording rejected applicant information.

Case F: Freddie

Freddie had been matched with Gil for almost three months. Freddie called his program coordinator, Chelsea, to say that his match was "not working." Chelsea was pleased to hear from him: Freddie had been extremely responsive during the application process, but he had been difficult to contact since being matched with his mentee. When questioned, Freddie said that Gil was too private and that his family only allowed the pair to spend the recommended three hours a week together. Freddie explained that he had more time to devote to a young person and that Gil and his family were not taking full advantage of his availability. He also questioned whether Gil really needed a mentor since his mother and grandfather were both in his life. Even as Chelsea tried to learn more about the past three months, Freddie's replies were brief, and he insisted that he did not want to continue mentoring Gil. The pair had not attended any group activities, so none of the staff had seen them interact with each other. Chelsea had spoken regularly with Gil, but he was not very communicative over the phone. Chelsea told Freddie that it was nearly time for the pair's three-month review, so they could plan it a little early in order to put closure on the relationship. She would pick up Gil the next day and bring him to the office. There, she would meet with Gil and Freddie separately and then together. During the course of her three-month discussion with Gil, he described his mentor as "weird but nice." In listening to the activities the pair had done together, Chelsea began to have concerns about their interactions and solitary activities. She carefully introduced the idea that maybe Freddie and Gil would be better matches for somebody else. At this comment, Gil smiled and seemed relieved. After then meeting with Freddie and completing the agency's three-month review procedures, the session concluded as Chelsea met with both Freddie and Gil and described how the pair had worked hard to get to know each other, but that sometimes mentors and mentees are not quite the right match for each other. She thanked them both for their honesty, their time, and their commitment to getting to know each other.

Red Flags and Informed Intuition

Freddie's sudden change in communication with The Agency offered a possible red flag regarding his relationship with his mentee. Child molesters groom their victims over time, breaking down barriers and gaining their trust. If a child is not responsive to the child molester's advances, he or she may request another mentee. This may have been the case with Freddie, particularly given his suggestions for another mentee. The solitary activities and length of activities Freddie planned were problematic. Given Freddie's comments, it appears that Gil's mother did not want him to spend too much time with Freddie; if Chelsea had followed up with Gil's mother, she may have found that this was because of her discomfort with the mentor.

Agency Shortfalls

While coordinating so many mentees, mentors, and meetings, it is not unusual for one relationship to go untracked, particularly if the program coordinator has repeatedly left voice messages or e-mails for the mentor. In this case, Chelsea followed through on her responsibility to contact the mentee, but Gil's minimal feedback and Freddie's failure to communicate might have benefited from a visit to see Gil in person. Gil's mother and grandfather might also have helped to shed light on how the relationship was progressing. The Agency had implemented useful program procedures, offering opportunities for staff to easily intervene or simply gather additional details. To ensure the continued safety of participants, The Agency should monitor each program coordinator's caseload so that it does not exceed the number described by the mentoring field's recommended best practices.[106] Further, in speaking with Gil at their three-month meeting together, Chelsea could have asked Gil the more open-ended question of whether he thought that Freddie might be a good mentor for someone else. By asking this question, Chelsea could hopefully garner information on whether Gil thought that Freddie was not a good mentor, or if Freddie was just not right for him.

Did You Know?

Informed Intuition: Just as staff can be trained to develop Informed Intuition, they should also recognize that parents and guardians often have similar intuition. Concerns for their child's safety may be reflected in their reactions to their child's mentor. Staff should utilize the resource of family members, gauging whether their discomfort or unease with a mentor is related to a relationship that they find threatening to their role as a parent or caregiver … or whether the mentor "gives them the creeps." In either case, staff must intervene in support of the child.

---

[106] North, D., Sherk, J., and Strother, J. (2002). *Starting a Mentoring Program. Folsom*, CA: The EMT (Evaluation Management Training) Group, Inc. P. 2.

Conclusion

Once Freddie finally contacted her, Chelsea's quick response in planning a meeting helped her gather more information about the pair. Based primarily on Gil's feedback and reactions, Chelsea was able to facilitate an ending to the relationship rather than encouraging Freddie to continue trying to connect with Gil. Gil was successfully rematched several weeks later and completed a full year with his new mentor. The Agency has no plans to rematch Freddie.

PART III
Child Molestation Prevention: Tools and Resources

CHAPTER 8:
Fingerprinting

Every 11.5 hours,
a registered sex offender attempted to
obtain a position at a nonprofit.[107]

Both state- and federal-level background checks should be part of every organization's basic volunteer screening. Approximately 5.6 million Americans have ever served time in state or federal prison,[108] and an estimated 6.6% of Americans will serve time in prison during their lifetime.[109] Two-thirds of convicted rape and sexual assault offenders serving time in state prisons reported that their victims were under the age of 18, and 58% of those (nearly 4 in 10 imprisoned violent sex offenders) stated that their victims were aged 12 or younger.[110] Of offenders serving time for sexual assault convictions, 8 out of 10 had committed their crime against a victim under age 18.[111] Of offenders who had raped a child under the age of 12, 90% knew the child they abused.[112] Disturbingly, approximately 60% of sex offenders released from prison had victimized a child ages 13 or younger,[113] and 60% of convicted sex offenders are on parole or probation.[114]

---

[107] The Importance of Background Screening for Nonprofits: An Updated Briefing. April 2008. Alpharetta, Georgia: Choice Point Inc.

[108] Bureau of Justice Statistics. Criminal Offender Statistics. Retrieved December 9, 2005, from http://www.ojp.usdoj.gov/bjs/abstract/piusp01.htm

[109] Bureau of Justice Statistics. Criminal Offender Statistics. Retrieved December 9, 2005, from http://www.ojp.usdoj.gov/bjs/crimoff.htm

[110] Bureau of Justice Statistics. Criminal Offender Statistics. Retrieved December 9, 2005, from http://www.ojp.usdoj.gov/bjs/abstract/soo.htm

[111] Bureau of Justice Statistics. Criminal Offender Statistics. Retrieved December 9, 2005, from http://www.ojp.usdoj.gov/bjs/abstract/cvvoatv.htm

[112] Bureau of Justice Statistics. Criminal Offender Statistics. Retrieved December 9, 2005, from http://www.ojp.usdoj.gov/bjs/abstract/soo.htm

[113] Bureau of Justice Statistics. Criminal Offender Statistics. Retrieved December 9, 2005, from http://www.ojp.usdoj.gov/bjs/crimoff.htm

[114] Bureau of Justice Statistics. Criminal Offender Statistics. Retrieved December 9, 2005, from http://www.ojp.usdoj.gov/bjs/crimoff.htm

These statistics demonstrate a clear and present need for fingerprinting and national database verification as a minimal level of screening necessary for any organization which pairs children with mentors. Securing a criminal background check prior to a mentor's acceptance is critical, so that the safety of our most vulnerable youth is not jeopardized.

A Case Study
Provided by a Mentoring Program

We were having a hard time finding enough mentors before the start of our program and needed to match students with mentors before the match-day meeting. We decided to go ahead and match a student and a mentor together before the mentor's background clearance had come through the sheriff's department. We did this with the understanding that until the clearance came through, this mentor and student would be required to meet at our office under our supervision. The mentor and student met during the match-day meeting and hit if off. It was almost a week or two later that we received word from the sheriff's department that the mentor did not clear. She had had a prior conviction on her record for Driving Under the Influence and was not cleared to work with minors because of this. It then had to be explained to the student that the mentor was not able to continue in our program and that we were going to have to mentor her ourselves. This was very disappointing to the student initially. Although ultimately the student was very pleased with the support she received from our staff, this example proved to us the importance of obtaining clearances prior to matching students with their mentors.

FBI Fingerprint Checks

Unless a program is operated by a law enforcement agency, programs cannot request or directly receive FBI criminal history information. Youth-serving organizations can go through their state's repository to obtain an FBI check. Your state's attorney general website can guide you with this process. Some programs work with their local law enforcement agencies as well. Programs should expect to pay between $18 and $75 to obtain an FBI check.[115] Further information on this topic can be accessed at http://www.fbi.gov/about-us/cjis/criminal-history-summary-checks.

---

[115] Obtaining FBI Fingerprint Checks. Retrieved December 16, 2014 from
https://www.nationalserviceresources.gov/files/memo_obtainingfbifingerprintchecks_final_20140202_0.pdf

State and Local Criminal History Registry Checks

Most local law enforcement agencies offer fingerprinting services for a fee. In some states, the statewide repository offers an electronic fingerprinting network, or IAFIS/Integrated Automated Fingerprint Identification System. Response time to the contributing agency may be as little as two hours. Your state's attorney general website will have comprehensive information about this service and process. Every state will have unique procedures.

For illustrative purposes, consider the state of California. The California Department of Justice (DOJ) is mandated to maintain the statewide criminal record repository for the state of California. In this capacity, sheriff, police and probation departments, district attorney offices, and courts submit arrest and corresponding disposition information. The DOJ uses this information to compile records of arrest and prosecution, known as "RAP sheets," for individuals and disseminates the information for law enforcement and regulatory (employment and licensing) purposes. RAP sheets are based upon fingerprint submissions, and therefore positively identified biometrically, a process by which a person's unique identity is confirmed.

Authorized by California statute, the DOJ has processed State of California and Federal Bureau of Investigation (FBI) fingerprint-based background checks for decades. If an FBI criminal background check is requested, the fingerprint images are forwarded to the FBI to perform a fingerprint-based search of records in the national criminal history database. If the applicant's fingerprints match fingerprints in the national criminal history database, the FBI sends the DOJ a cumulative RAP sheet that contains criminal history information from any states or federal agencies that have reported the information to the FBI. If there is not a matching disposition for every out-of-state or federal arrest, the DOJ is again mandated by statute to perform the "genuine effort" to obtain the missing disposition information, just as with California arrests that are missing disposition information. Once the "genuine effort" is fulfilled, a DOJ technician must review the updated Rap sheet and prepare the background check response according to the statutory dissemination criterion.

There are over 40,000 agencies in California authorized to perform background checks. DOJ technicians process approximately 2 million state level background checks and 1.2 million federal level background checks annually.[116]

---

[116] Fingerprint Background Checks. Retrieved December 16, 2014 from oag.ca.gov/fingerprints.

Limitations of Fingerprint Background Checks

The limitations of background checks are disconcerting: "Only 1 in 150 deviant episodes actually lead to arrest."[117] In a study by E. Brongersma, fewer than 5% of 647 child molestations studied were ever reported to police. Brongersma reports that sexual offenders have bragged "1 unlawful sexual act with a minor in 3,000 is discovered, tried, and results in a sentence."[118] The use of background checks by mentoring agencies is also hampered by the voluntary nature of Volunteers for Children Act: there are inconsistencies in states' use of the law and in mentoring agencies' perception of the importance of background checks. It is clear that the frequency of conviction for child molestation is exceedingly low. A molester may affect the lives of hundreds of children before he or she appears in a Sexual Offender Registry. Further, glitches in background checking systems can sometimes cause important information to be lost. While computerization has made recent criminal convictions show up fairly quickly within the system doing a check, older convictions might not be as obvious.[119] Therefore, while background checks are a must to prevent gross oversight (and legal culpability), it is critical to remember that background checks are not NEARLY enough to guarantee the safety of children.

---

[117] Abel, G., Becker, J., Mittleman, M., Rouleau, J., and Murphy, W. (1987). Self-reported sex crimes of nonincarcerated paraphiliacs. Journal of Interpersonal Violence, 2(1), March. Pp. 3-25.

[118] Brongersma, E. (1991). Boy-lovers and their influence on boys: Distorted research and anecdotal observations. Journal of Homosexuality, 20(1/2). P. 154.

[119] Limitations on Background Checks. Retrieved December 16, 2014 from http://www.ehow.com/info_7745664_limitations-background-checks.html

Background Check Conversation with John Patterson, Senior Program Director, The Nonprofit Risk Management Center[120]

The Nonprofit Risk Management Center receives many questions concerning the screening of staff and volunteers using criminal history record checks. Criminal history record checks are important risk management tools but must not replace other risk management strategies designed to lessen the opportunity for abuse of vulnerable service recipients. No background check is perfect and the fact that an applicant appears to have a clean record is not predictive of future behavior. The following are some of the more frequently asked questions concerning criminal history record checks.

Q: Are we required to conduct criminal history record checks?

A: The answer to this question depends upon the nature of the services you offer and the jurisdiction in which you offer them. For most nonprofit organizations offering services to children, dependent elderly, or people with disabilities, the answer is that there are no *legal* requirements for you to conduct criminal history record checks. The usual exceptions to this are services for which licenses are required. For example, childcare programs licensed by the state may be required to conduct criminal history record checks on their staff. In additional to legal requirements, there may be *contractual* requirements for your employees and volunteers to have criminal history record checks. For example, your insurer may require criminal history record checks in order to obtain sexual molestation liability insurance coverage. If you fail to conduct the record checks, the insurer would be able to refuse molestation claims because the organization failed in its contractual obligations. Another contractual requirement may be in the usage agreement for certain kinds of facilities. For example, a sports program using a municipal park may be required by the municipality to conduct background checks of the coaches as a condition of use for the park. Another example of a contractual requirement to conduct criminal history record checks may be found in

---

[120] Patterson, John. Senior Program Director, The Nonprofit Risk Management Center (personal correspondence, Fall 2004).

the language of funding agencies and organizations. Funders for your organization's services may make financial support conditional upon conducting criminal history record checks of the organization's employees and volunteers. Organizations should review their relevant local and state laws and regulations, licensing requirements, insurance policies, other contracts, and grant documents to ascertain any requirements for criminal history record checks.

Q: If we are required to conduct criminal history record checks or if our organization has adopted a policy requiring criminal history record checks, how can we obtain criminal history record checks?

A: There are two basic sources for criminal history record checks: official criminal history record repositories located in each state and private vendors. State laws and regulations govern access to records in official record repositories. State repositories are also the gateway into the Federal Bureau of Investigation's (FBI) criminal history records. State repositories also maintain sex offender registries, many of which are available online to the public.

Q: Are all criminal history record checks the same?

A: Criminal history record checks are not all the same. The primary variables are whether it is name-based or fingerprint-based. In addition, the databases used for the record checks are not the same. Most states permit access to their criminal history records for nonprofits to screen employees and volunteers. The Attorney General's office in each state makes this information available. Many states permit name-based record checks in which the identification parameters used are the individual's name, sex, and date of birth. Some states require that fingerprints be used for identification purposes. Fingerprints are the only practical way to ensure that the person being screened and the record match. Name-based searches often result in false matches - especially for individuals who have common names. In addition name-based searches may result in individuals beating the system by giving false identifying information. All FBI criminal history record checks require submitting a complete set of readable fingerprints. Private vendors use a combination of name, date of birth, and social security number to identify search subjects. Most will include individuals in their reports with two of the three identifiers matching. Similar to the state record check, this may result in a significant number of false identifications with individuals having common names. Name-based checks also yield false negatives in which individuals who should have been identified are placed in positions of trust working with vulnerable service recipients. The scope of the record check is also determined by the method used. Checks performed by state criminal history record repositories usually are limited to offenses committed within that state. The FBI national record check includes offenses committed throughout the nation and either reported to the FBI or identified through the FBI's recent Interstate Identification Index (III) system. Private vendors access public records — most often courthouse records — and create their own proprietary databases. The databases may be nation-wide in scope but limited to those areas in which the vendor has conducted business.

Q: Our organization wants to initiate criminal history record checks. What do we need to do to get started?

A: Remember that criminal history record checking is a process that yields information. The central question is how is your organization is going to use the information obtained through the record checks. After considering your employees' and volunteers' specific responsibilities, the organization needs to decide what offenses will disqualify applicants from positions in your organization. Most organizations permanently disqualify anyone convicted of sex-related crimes, violent crimes, and crimes in which children were involved. For other kinds of crimes, factors such as the age of the individual at the time of the offense, how long ago the offense occurred, the person's attitude about the offense, and the person's lifestyle since the offense may be considered.

Q: Who should have access to the information we receive from criminal history record checks?

A: It is important that information received as a result of a criminal history record check be handled to preserve its confidentiality. The executive director or a staff member designated by the executive director should be the only person with access to the information. Individuals' criminal history records should not be the topic of staff discussions beyond a limited number who have a need to know.

Third Party Vendors

There are many third party vendors who will conduct background checks for an organization. These are often more costly, but may save time and yield quicker results. In researching third party vendors as an option, ensure that the information they receive is thorough and matches what you are able to legally receive as a youth-serving agency. Be sure to understand any obligations that you have to applicants as well.

CHAPTER 9:
Sexual Offender Registry

In recent decades, sex offenders have been the targets of some of the most far-reaching and novel crime legislation in the U.S. Two key innovations have been registration and notification laws which, respectively, require that convicted sex offenders provide valid contact information to law enforcement authorities, and that information on sex offenders be made public. There is a scarcity of good research on the effectiveness of the Sexual Offender Registry. A few states, including Arkansas, New Jersey, and New York, have conducted research on their impact. One study by Prescott and Rockoff used detailed information on the timing and scope of changes in state law to study how registration and notification affected the frequency of sex offenses and the incidence of offenses across victims. They found evidence that registration reduces the frequency of sex offenses by providing law enforcement with information on local sex offenders.

They correctly predicted, however, that this decrease in crime was concentrated among "local" victims (e.g., friends, acquaintances, neighbors), while there was little evidence of a decrease in crimes against strangers. They also found evidence that community notification deters first-time sex offenses, but increases recidivism by registered offenders due to a change in the relative utility of legal and illegal behavior. This finding is consistent with work by criminologists suggesting that notification may increase recidivism by imposing social and financial costs on registered sex offenders and making non-criminal activity relatively less attractive. They regarded this latter finding as potentially important, given that the purpose of community notification is to reduce recidivism.[121]

---

[121] Prescott, J.J. and Rockoff, Jonah E. (February 2008). Do Sex Offender Registration and Notification Laws Affect Criminal Behavior? NBER Working Paper No. w13803. Available at SSRN: http://ssrn.com/abstract=1100584

Megan's Law

The federal version of Megan's Law was enacted on May 17th, 1996. Megan's Law was named after seven-year-old Megan Kanka, a New Jersey girl who was raped and killed by a known child molester who had moved across the street from her home without her parents' knowledge. Megan's Law mandates that every state develop a procedure for notifying residents of sex offenders residing there. Each state differs on how they report the information, but the National Alert Registry has combined all of the states' information in to one database.

One of the important aspects of Megan's Law is the requirement of convicted sex offenders to notify authorities of their current address. Every time a convicted sex offender moves they are required to notify the local police of their new address. This allows the public to know where the sex offenders live at all times. However, this requirement is not always permanent and many convicted sex offenders are only required to report updates of their address for 10 years.

To find out more about how your state allows access to data on Megan's Law offenders, contact your state's Office of the Attorney General. The Klaas Kids Foundation offers links to databases in each state at www.klaaskids.org. Links are also provided on www.registeredoffenderslist.org, www.kidslivesafe.com, www.fbi.gov/scams-safety/registry, and www.meganslaw.com.

Dru Sjodin
National Sex Offender Public Website

The National Sex Offender Public Registry (NSOPR) was first established in 2005. On July 27, 2006, President George W. Bush signed into law the Adam Walsh Child Protection and Safety Act. This act included Dru's Law, which, among other things, changed the name of the National Sex Offender Public Registry (NSOPR) to the Dru Sjodin National Sex Offender Public Website (NSOPW), which provides information to the public on the whereabouts of registered sex offenders regardless of state boundaries. 22-year-old college student Dru Sjodin of Grand Forks, North Dakota, was a young woman who was kidnapped and murdered by a sex offender who was registered in Minnesota.

NSOPW is the only U.S. government website that links public state, territorial, and tribal sex offender registries from one national search site, www.nsopw.gov. Parents, employers, and other concerned residents can utilize the website's search tool to identify location information on sex offenders residing, working, and attending school not only in their own neighborhoods but in other nearby states and communities. In addition, the website provides visitors with information about sexual abuse and how to protect themselves and loved ones from potential victimization.

NSOPW's advanced search tool provides information about sex offenders through a number of search options:

- Search by name nationally or with an individual jurisdiction
- Search by address (if provided by jurisdiction)
- Search by zip code
- Search by county (if provided by jurisdiction)
- Search by city/town (if provided by jurisdiction)

NSOPW presents the most up-to-date information as provided by each jurisdiction. Information is hosted by each jurisdiction, not by NSOPW or the federal government. The search criteria available for searches are limited to what each individual jurisdiction may provide.[122]

---

[122] U.S. Department of Justice NSOPW. Retrieved December 15, 2014, from www.nsopw.com

Limitations of Using Sex Offender Registries

Checking sex offender registries is better than no record check at all, but they do have some serious limitations. Most states have sex offender registries accessible to the public via the Internet. The theory behind sex offender registries is that individuals convicted for sex-related crimes must register each time they move and this enables law enforcement agencies and members of the public to know when a dangerous offender is in their area. Some states limit the publicly accessible list to only the most serious of all sex offenders so failure to appear on these registries would not mean that the individual is not a sex offender. The large number of sex offenders who fail to register in a timely fashion hampers the effectiveness of sex offender registries. According to klaaskids.org, as of September 15, 2014 there are nearly 750,000 individuals registered on the Sex Offender Registry. For states that report non-registration data, the number of non-compliant individuals ranges from 2% to 22%.

The quality of the information is questionable, so not having information on an individual does not necessarily mean that the individual has not committed a sex-related offense. Having said that, sex offender registries may be useful for supplementing state record checks as they may include individuals convicted of sex offenses in another state. The key to using sex offender registries effectively is understanding the parameters used by the state when listing offenders in its registry. Most states include this information on their websites.[123]

---

[123] Patterson, John. Senior Program Director, The Nonprofit Risk Management Center (personal correspondence, Fall 2004).

CHAPTER 10:
Sexual Abuse Reporting

Mandatory reporting of child abuse, including sexual abuse, should be a part of both organizational policies as well as the Mentor Code of Conduct. Staff and mentors should be trained on these procedures and understand their respective roles. Every state has a mandatory reporting process of suspected child abuse and/or neglect. To find out details of mandatory reporting laws in each state, visit the website for National Clearinghouse on Child Abuse and Neglect: www.calib.com/nccanch.

Handling Sexual Abuse Disclosure [124]

How do you talk to a child you suspect is being abused? You prepare to talk to a child by becoming as knowledgeable as possible about the issue you are going to discuss before it becomes an issue. Rape crisis teams, domestic violence services, and victim witness programs around the country provide no-cost training and support for those professionals whose clients might be dealing with issues of sexual violence. It is also important to acknowledge and name sexual violence when it occurs. Regardless of how much or how little force or battery was used,

---

[124] Keele, Lorey. (2004). Redwood Community Action Agency Northcoast Mentor Program and Council. Unpublished manuscript.

abuse of children that incorporates touching of genitals either of the child or perpetrator IS sexual violence. The child has very little to no power or control of the situation; the rights of the child are violated.

People with past experiences or issues that would impede them from asking or inquiring into possible abuse of a child should NOT be the staff person talking with the child, parent, or mentor. Often those adults who have personally experienced abuse can still be traumatized or angry and might carry residual effects of the incident that would prevent them from being effective in discussing the issue with clients. Staff whose family member/s or others close to them who have been accused of child abuse can be unconsciously putting up walls or blocking discussion of possible abuse by those wanting to ask questions or express concerns.

One of the most potentially damaging issues for children who disclose abuse is not being heard or believed or even blamed during or after a disclosure. If any of these reactions occur, children can carry the effects of those responses long into adulthood, if not for the rest of their lives. Some adults who reported or tried to disclose abuse as a child but experienced negative reactions can feel further damage, which is clearly harmful and, furthermore, can compound the violation or abuse. Although children can know that the abuse is bad or wrong, when the responsible or trusting adult betrays them, it can increase their sense of isolation and trauma. Organizations are obligated to set policy regarding disclosure of abuse and provide staff training that supports those policies to protect the children in your program. This is an issue of liability and risk management for organizations serving children. The clearer you are about dealing with these issues, the more you reduce your risk as an organization and, most importantly, for the children you serve. Discuss this issue of reporting between staff so that everyone understands the process.

The following are steps for setting up an appropriate and safe environment for talking with a child:
1. Meet or talk away from his/her family or friends.
2. Meet or talk at a time when neither of you feels rushed or distracted.
3. Meet or talk in a space that provides confidentiality – talking to a child while he/she is at home where the abuser might be could put that child in further danger.

4. Allow time for normal conversation.
5. When the appropriate time arises, you may want to explain to the child that you have concerns. For example:
    a. "When I saw you last week at the picnic, you looked sad and uncomfortable. Was anything wrong?" Avoid asking leading questions of a child.
    b. "How do you feel about your mentor? Do you feel safe with your mentor? How do you like being with your mentor?"
    c. "I heard that you and your mentor went biking on Sunday and you were angry when you came home. Would you like to talk about what made you angry?"

NEVER put words into a child's mouth. Always use open-ended questions. Let them label their own feelings. It is okay to say what you are seeing or feeling. You might have a feeling that something is upsetting a child. It might be something that is innocent, such as mentor pregnancy or a family move.

If a mentee discloses abuse, you must let him/her know that he/she is not to blame. A child does not ask to be abused, but she/he may have received the message from the perpetrator that she/he did something to warrant the abuse. Assure the child that the perpetrator, adult or teen, is responsible for the abuse.

A difficult part of hearing a reportable incident is telling the child that you must report the abuse to the authorities. During the initial program orientation session with the child, parent/s and mentor should discuss what happens if an issue of abuse arises and particularly the respective parties' roles as mandated reporters. Once a child discloses, you can refer back to that discussion. Let the child know that his/her safety is most important and that you will need to get help from child protective service professionals and/or the police authorities who will talk with the child about what happened.

Once a child discloses:
1. Again, do not put words into their mouths.
2. Repeat back what you are hearing with the words THEY are using, even if they are pointing to a part of the body that they are identifying incorrectly.

Sometimes perpetrators mislabel body parts while molesting a child for the purpose of making their disclosure less credible or seem untrue.

3. If you sense a child is having difficulty talking to you, sit down with drawing materials or a toy and let them know that you will help them with any problem they are having.

4. Be direct. Ask gently but directly if the child is having a problem he/she needs help with.

5. Stay with the child. Don't disconnect or allow yourself to be distracted by phone calls, interruptions, or writing down what she/he is saying. Disclosing is traumatic for anyone, much less a child. No matter how calm or controlled the child looks, he/she is likely to be experiencing fear, humiliation, and a sense of responsibility for the abuse.

6. Do not show shock, disgust, or anger. Children are very intuitive and are reading your every move and response. They can be influenced by your reactions and actions. They could change their statements or become unresponsive as a result.

7. **Do not** promise not to tell.

8. Let the child know what to expect; if you don't know, say so. Don't give a child false hope. Don't assume that because another known case of child abuse ended a certain way that his/her situation will result in the same outcome. Again, you can do additional harm by what the child might see as betrayal. Let the child know he/she can expect you to be supportive and helpful.

9. Assure the child that they are not in trouble. Children may feel responsible for the abuse. They may believe that they are (or will be) in trouble and might even think they will go to jail.

Disclosure by a child could mean that you do not release them to anyone except child protective services or law enforcement. Let the child know that you are going to call for help and ask if it is okay to bring in another staff member to sit with the child. The child might not want you to leave the room. You can ask that another staff member make the initial call. If you have no other option, it is usually better to make the initial call in front of the child than to leave him/her alone.

If the perpetrator is in the home, you must call child protective services immediately but not in the presence of the child. Call your local child protective service's 24-hour hotline if it is not during normal business hours.

CHAPTER 11:
Mentor Code of Conduct

The Mentor Code of Conduct is a set of policies to which participating mentors agree to abide. These topics are typically introduced throughout the mentor screening process, with mentor applicants signing the Mentor Code of Conduct document during the volunteer training session or just prior to his or her match with a mentee. This document can assist individuals in successfully fulfilling their responsibilities as a mentor. It can also assist program staff by highlighting areas of concern if a mentor fails to adhere to these policies. While the Mentor Code of Conduct should include a range of topics which will ensure the safety and well-being of mentees, several topics hold particular relevance for preventing child sexual abuse. These topics include

1. Gift-giving,
2. Self-disclosure,
3. Keeping secrets,
4. Alcohol and drug use,
5. Discussions about sex, and
6. Overnights.

Programs should make sure that mentors thoroughly understand the Mentor Code of Conduct. Code items can be effectively addressed during volunteer training role-play scenarios or discussions. For each topic, firm and explicit conditions should be established, with clear consequences for infractions.

Programs should seek the advice of their legal counsel in designing their Mentor Code of Conduct.

For more in-depth background information on program policy areas which should be addressed by a Mentor Code of Conduct, a variety of online manuals are available:

Generic Mentoring Program Policy and Procedure Manual
Hamilton Fish Institute on School and Community Violence and The National Mentoring Center at Northwest Regional Educational Laboratory
http://www.mentoring.org/images/uploads/MentoringPolicy.pdf

Risk Management for Mentoring Programs
The EMT Group: Dustianne North and Jerry Sherk
http://www.vamentoring.org/images/uploads/resources/EMT_Risk_Management_f
or_Mentoring_Programs.pdf

Sample
Mentor Code of Conduct

The following is a Code of Conduct required of all mentors in **THE AGENCY**. Please read and sign below. If you have any questions, contact **YOUR PROGRAM COORDINATOR**.

1. You and **THE AGENCY** staff members are the only individuals allowed to operate the car in which your mentee rides. Always ensure that your mentee is wearing a seatbelt in the car, and obey all traffic laws. You may only take your mentee on a motorcycle/airplane if you have obtained permission directly from the parent/guardian. If your spouse/partner would like to drive your mentee, s/he must submit her/his driving record and proof of auto insurance to **THE AGENCY**.

2. Maintain liability insurance on your car throughout the duration of your commitment as a mentor. You and your mentee may be covered by **THE AGENCY**'s insurance should something happen; however, anyone else not involved with **THE AGENCY** is your liability.

3. If you are running late, call your mentee to let her/him know what time you will be there.

4. Always inform your mentee's parent/guardian of your plans and what time you expect to return your mentee home, so they can arrange to be there when you arrive. Let the parent/guardian know that you cannot leave their child at an empty house. Discuss these arrangements when you pick up your mentee. If you are running late, call the parent/guardian as soon as possible.

5. Never use alcohol or drugs when you are with your mentee. Never offer your mentee alcohol, tobacco, or other drugs.

6. Never ask your mentee to keep a secret.

7. If you suspect abuse or neglect of your mentee, discuss this with **YOUR PROGRAM COORDINATOR** immediately.

8. Corporal punishment and physical discipline of your mentee are not permitted even if the parent/guardian gives you permission. Discuss an appropriate means of setting goals and limits with **YOUR PROGRAM COORDINATOR**.

9. Respect the privacy and personal boundaries of your mentee. Inappropriate behavior, such as sexual relationships, abuse, or molestation, is not permitted.

10. **THE AGENCY** does not allow overnight visits with the exception of **THE AGENCY** supervised group activities such as ski trips and camping.

11. Your mentee is never to be left in anyone else's care, including boyfriends, girlfriends, husbands, wives, or friends.

I agree to abide by **THE AGENCY**'s Code of Conduct.

Mentor: _____
             Printed name   Signature   Date

Coordinator: _____
             Printed name   Signature   Date

Copyright © Friends for Youth 2014

CHAPTER 12:
Resources

The Diana Screen:
Online Risk Management Tool

The Diana Screen is a computer-based volunteer risk management/pre-hire instrument that has proven effective at keeping children and teens safe from sexual abuse and sexual boundary violations by screening the general population to identify individuals who are a sexual risk to children. Scientifically validated and backed by over 20 years of research, The Diana Screen is an online instrument of 120 questions that potential mentors complete. It utilizes three measures to assess sexual risk in candidates by screening for men and women who have beliefs about the rights of adults to have sexual contact with children and teens. It also identifies candidates who will not protect children from other adults/older children who may be sexually inappropriate and will not protect your organization from these sexually inappropriate adults/older children. Further information about The Diana Screen can be found at www.dianascreen.com.

Other Testing Tools

There are other psychometric and psychological tests that are often used by organizations, particularly in employment situations. If you choose to utilize one of these measures, ensure that appropriately trained staff and/or consultants conduct and analyze the results. More importantly, make sure that your selection of a particular instrument is connected to the qualities that you are seeking in your mentors.

Publications
Containing Child Molestation Prevention Information

Publications containing the most thorough research and recommendations include:

Arévalo, Elsy, and Cooper, Becky. (2002). *Running a Safe and Effective Mentoring Program.* **Los Altos, CA: Friends for Youth, Inc.**
This manual is designed to help readers increase the effectiveness of their mentoring programs by providing a systematic way of implementing mentoring best practices into their services. The manual covers key areas such as volunteer recruitment, screening, training, and evaluation.
Available for order at energizeinc.com.

Kremer, Sarah and Cooper, Becky. (2014). *Mentor Screening and Youth Protection* **(Chapter 28) in Handbook of Youth Mentoring Second Edition, Edited by David L. DuBois and Michael J. Karcher. Thousand Oaks, CA: Sage Publications.**
This chapter reviews research on mentor screening and youth protection in mentoring programs, providing recommended tools and approaches for mentoring programs based on this research.

Groth, A. Nicholas. (1979). *Men Who Rape: The Psychology of the Offender.* **Plenum Press.**
Dr. Groth pioneered work on developing typologies of individuals who sexually abuse children. His profile of the "Fixated" Child Sexual Abuser has informed screening training on techniques, patterns, and other issues that drive the offender.

van Dam, Carla. (2001). *Identifying child molesters: Preventing child sexual abuse by recognizing the patterns of the offenders.* **Binghamton, NY: The Haworth Press.**

van Dam, Carla. (2006). *The socially skilled child molester: Differentiating the guilty from the falsely accused.* **Binghamton, NY: The Haworth Maltreatment and Trauma Press.**
Over the course of her career, Dr. van Dam has worked with organizations and communities to prevent child sexual abuse. She has provided training on prevention strategies to mentoring and other community organizations.

Additional sources of materials that programs can reference include:

- *Supervision of Children and Teens Never Includes Sex* brochure from the Alliance of Nonprofits for Insurance
  http://www.oursharedresources.com/Resource/ViewResource/592

- *The Effects of Childhood Stress on Health Across the Lifespan* report from the Centers for Disease Control and Prevention
  http://www.cdc.gov/ncipc/pub-res/pdf/Childhood_Stress.pdf

- *Child Molesters: A Behavioral Analysis (For Law Enforcement Officers Investigating the Sexual Exploitation of Children by Acquaintance Molesters)* report from the Office of Juvenile Justice and Delinquency Prevention and the National Center for Missing & Exploited Children
  http://www.missingkids.com/en_US/publications/NC70.pdf

- *Preventing Child Sexual Abuse Within Youth-serving Organizations* report from the Centers for Disease Control and Prevention
  http://www.cdc.gov/ViolencePrevention/pdf/PreventingChildSexualAbuse-a.pdf

- *Screening Volunteers to Prevent Child Sexual Abuse: A Community Guide for Youth Organizations* report from the National Collaboration for Youth
  https://www.nationalserviceresources.org/library/items/r0872

- *Who's Lending a Hand? A National Survey of Nonprofit Volunteer Screening Practices* report from The National Center for Victims of Crime
  http://www.ncdsv.org/images/NCVC_Who%27sLendingAHand_2008.pdf

- *More Than a Matter of Trust: Managing the Risks of Mentoring* from the Nonprofit Risk Management Center
  http://nonprofitrisk.org/store/pub_detail.asp?id=10

- MENTOR/National Mentoring Partnership's *Elements of Effective Practice for Mentoring*, Third Edition
  http://www.mentoring.org/program_resources/elements_and_toolkits

- National Mentoring Center/Mentoring Resource Center, including *The U.S. Department of Education Mentoring Program's Guide to Screening and Background Checks* http://educationnorthwest.org/sites/default/files/resources/screening.pdf and their Fact Sheet 11: Managing Risk After the Match Is Made http://educationnorthwest.org/sites/default/files/resources/factsheet11.pdf

- *Prevent Child Abuse America series on Sexual Abuse* http://www.safersociety.org/uploads/WP071-Prevent-Child-Abuse.pdf

- *Kidpower* offering personal safety, confidence, advocacy, and self-protection skills for all ages and abilities http://www.kidpower.org

- *Darkness to Light,* Stewards of Children curriculum is an evidence-based adult-focused child sexual abuse prevention training program available in instructor-led and online formats. According to Darkness to Light, the Stewards of Children program is the only adult-focused child sexual abuse prevention program proven effective in increasing knowledge, improving attitudes, and changing participant's child-protective behaviors over the long term. http://www.darkness2light.org

- *Developmental Experiences of Child Sexual Abusers and Rapists* by Simons, Wurtele, & Durham http://eric.ed.gov/?id=EJ797436

- *Research Summary: Adults at Risk of Sexually Abusing Children* from Stop It Now! Minnesota http://www.stopitnow.org/files/Ad_Release_Summary.pdf

- *Sexual Abuse by Educators and School Staff,* Virginia Department of Social Services, Child Protective Services Unit https://www.childwelfare.gov/can/statistics/stat_sexAbuse.cfm

Organizations Providing Child Molestation Prevention Resources

Abel Screening, Inc. and The Diana Screen

800-806-2235

www.DIANASCREEN.com

Abel Screening, Inc. developed The Diana Screen, a simple, risk management tool that can be used to keep children safe. Twenty years in development, The Diana Screen is an online instrument of 120 questions that potential mentors complete. It utilizes three measures to assess sexual risk in candidates.

Childhelp USA®

800-4-A-CHILD (800-422-4453) (24-hour hotline)

www.childhelp.org

Childhelp USA serves abused children through supporting residential treatment facilities, group homes, child advocacy centers, child abuse prevention programs, and outreach. In addition, it sponsors a 24/7 Childhelp National Child Abuse Hotline.

Child Lures Prevention

802-985-8458

www.childluresprevention.com

Based on child safety expert Kenneth Wooden's research, the Child Lures Prevention site includes resources and articles for parents, professionals, children, educators, and communities on keeping children safe.

Child Molestation Research and Prevention Institute

404-872-5152

510- 808-0386

www.childmolestationprevention.org

CMRPI provides trainings, workshops, and lectures on primary and secondary prevention of child sexual abuse as well as provides educational materials for sale. Their website outlines "The Child Molestation Prevention Plan," a listing of "sex-specific therapy sites" in North America, and "Six Questions to Ask a Sex-Specific Therapist" before making an appointment, among other valuable resources. Visitors to the website may also access or download the "Abel and Harlow Child Molestation Prevention Study."

Child Welfare Information Gateway

800-394-3366

www.childwelfare.gov/can/

The Child Welfare Information Gateway (formerly known as the National Clearinghouse on Child Abuse and Neglect Information) is a national resource center for professionals and the public seeking information about child maltreatment. The Child Welfare Information Gateway collects and disseminates information about such topics as policy and legislation, treatment, prevention, research, public awareness, training, and education.

Future of Children

www.futureofchildren.org

The Future of Children provides extensive research and analysis to promote effective policies and programs for children by providing policymakers, service providers, and media representatives with timely, objective information based on available research. Issues that may be of particular interest include "Preventing Child Maltreatment," "Sexual Abuse of Children," and "Protecting Children from Abuse and Neglect," available using the site's 'Publication' function.

Leadership Council on Child Abuse and Interpersonal Violence

610-664-5007

www.leadershipcouncil.org or www.stopitnow.org

Formerly the Leadership Council on Mental Health, Justice, and the Media, the Council was founded in 1998 and is committed to providing professionals and laypersons with accurate, research-based information about a variety of mental health issues and to preserving society's commitment to protect its most vulnerable members. Their site contains research articles about the effects of child sexual abuse.

MaleSurvivor: National Organization Against Male Sexual Victimization

http://www.malesurvivor.org

MaleSurvivor is committed to preventing, healing, and eliminating all forms of sexual victimization of boys and men through treatment, research, education, advocacy, and activism. Their website provides resources and articles focused specifically on the sexual abuse of men and boys.

National Center for Missing and Exploited Children

800-THE-LOST (800-843-5678) (24-hour hotline)

703-224-2150

www.missingkids.com or www.cybertipline.com

The National Center for Missing & Exploited Children launched the CyberTipline in 1998 for online reporting of child sexual exploitation in cooperation with the Federal Bureau of Investigation, U.S. Immigration and Customs Enforcement (formerly the U.S. Customs Service), and the U.S. Postal Inspection Service. They have implemented many other safety programs as well.

National Center for Victims of Crime

202-467-8700

www.victimsofcrime.org

The National Center for Victims of Crime is a nonprofit organization advocating for all victims of crime. They educate child victims about their rights and the recent provisions that have been established to protect them. Their website has a link to a Connect Directory that helps victims locate service providers.

Friends for Youth Products and Services

To order, visit
www.friendsforyouth.org
or call (650) 368-4444

.

Products

Running a Safe and Effective Mentoring Program Manual

This how-to manual is designed to help increase the effectiveness of mentoring programs by providing a systematic way of incorporating mentoring best practices into services. Covering such key areas as volunteer recruitment, screening, training, and evaluation, the manual is based on mentoring research, best practices, information gathered from working with hundreds of mentoring programs, and over 3 decades of successfully mentoring youth.

Mentoring Activity Journal

Filled with creative and interactive activities, the Mentoring Activity Journal is a tool to help mentors and mentees develop and document their relationship. The Journal includes ideas for activities that mentors and mentees can do on their own, tips on getting to know each other and building their friendship, and structured activities that address key issues for both youth and mentors. Utilized over time, the Journal becomes a treasured book that mentors and mentees can keep for a lifetime of memories.

Connections Newsletter

Each quarterly Connections newsletter focuses on a specific mentoring model, practice, or relevant issue. Friends for Youth partners with fellow practitioners in the mentoring field to ensure that articles include new perspective and approaches.

SAFE (Screening Applicants for Effectiveness) **Manual**
The primary responsibility of any youth service provider is to ensure the safety and well-being of the children and youth in their program. SAFE (Screening Applicants for Effectiveness): Recommendations and Guidelines to Prevent Child Molestation covers all aspects of volunteer screening and monitoring to help keep youth safe. This manual includes research and statistics on the prevalence of sexual abuse, characteristics of child predators and their tactics, information about potential victims, and guidelines for programs to protect youth. A variety of experts and youth practitioners share their knowledge through case studies and tools for effective screening. This manual is a must-have for anyone who works with children and youth.

Services

Trainings
Friends for Youth's trainings are excellent resources for individuals and agencies that are designing and implementing effective youth mentoring programs. Friends for Youth's experienced presenters draw on their 35 years of success to help develop and improve programs.

Webinars
Friends for Youth's Mentoring Institute offers customized training created for programs, collaboratives, symposiums, or conferences that is delivered online. Webinars can be presented through a program's existing management system or can hosted by Friends for Youth. Online learning is becoming an increasingly easy format to save costs, save energy, and save the environment. It is also conducive to gathering staff to use existing meeting time for an informative session focused on areas most needed.

Conference
Presented bi-annually, Friends for Youth's Mentoring Conference brings together practitioners, researchers, mentors, mentees, community leaders, legislators, and corporate representatives. The workshops and keynote presentations facilitate attendees' enthusiasm, positive energy, eagerness to learn and share, and commitment to the mentoring field. Attendees from across the country, and even from a few other countries, join Friends for Youth to participate in the plenary and workshop sessions with focus, commitment, and thoughtfulness.